Better Homes and Gardens®

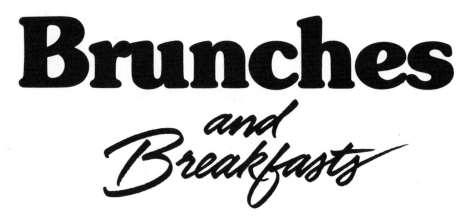

Brunches
and Breakfasts

Our seal assures you that every recipe in *Brunches and Breakfasts*
has been tested in the Better Homes and Gardens® Test Kitchen.
This means that each recipe is practical and reliable,
and meets our high standards of taste appeal.

BETTER HOMES AND GARDENS® BOOKS

Editor: Gerald M. Knox
Art Director: Ernest Shelton
Managing Editor: David A. Kirchner
Editorial Project Managers: Liz Anderson, James D. Blume,
    Marsha Jahns, Jennifer Speer Ramundt, Angela Renkoski

Department Head, Cook Books: Sharyl Heiken
Associate Department Heads: Sandra Granseth,
    Rosemary C. Hutchinson, Elizabeth Woolever
Senior Food Editors: Linda Henry, Marcia Stanley,
    Joyce Trollope
Associate Food Editors: Jennifer Darling, Heather Hephner,
    Mary Major, Mary Jo Plutt
Assistant Food Editor: Shelli McConnell
Test Kitchen: Director, Sharon Stilwell; Photo Studio Director,
    Janet Herwig; Home Economists: Kay Cargill, Marilyn Cornelius,
    Maryellyn Krantz, Lynelle Munn, Marge Steenson,
    Colleen Weeden

Associate Art Directors: Neoma Thomas, Linda Ford Vermie,
    Randall Yontz
Assistant Art Directors: Lynda Haupert, Harijs Priekulis,
    Tom Wegner
Graphic Designers: Mary Schlueter Bendgen, Mike Burns,
    Brian Wignall
Art Production: Director, John Berg; Associate, Joe Heuer;
    Office Manager, Michaela Lester

President, Book Group: Jeramy Lanigan
Vice President, Retail Marketing: Jamie L. Martin
Vice President, Administrative Services: Rick Rundall

BETTER HOMES AND GARDENS® MAGAZINE
President, Magazine Group: James A. Autry
Editorial Director: Doris Eby
Editorial Services Director: Duane L. Gregg
Food and Nutrition Editor: Nancy Byal

MEREDITH CORPORATION OFFICERS
Chairman of the Executive Committee: E. T. Meredith III
Chairman of the Board: Robert A. Burnett
President: Jack D. Rehm

BRUNCHES AND BREAKFASTS

Editor: Joyce Trollope
Editorial Project Manager: Liz Anderson
Contributing Graphic Designer: Patty Konecny
Electronic Text Processor: Paula Forest
Food Stylist: Janet Herwig
Contributing Photographers: M. Jensen Photography, Inc.,
    Scott Little

On the cover: *Shortcut Eggs Benedict* (see recipe, page 12)
    and *Citrus Eye-Opener* (see recipe, page 72)

Contents

Getting It Together

Good Morning! It's time to rise, shine, and start the day with an enjoyable, eye-opening meal! No matter whether you call it brunch or breakfast, you'll find deliciously appealing foods for the morning or midday in *Brunches and Breakfasts*.

Page through the book and choose from dozens of great-tasting recipes—from fabulous fruit combos and mouth-watering egg dishes to perfect pancakes and rolls. Plus there are vegetables, salads, and beverages to round out your meals. We've even planned three menus for brunch-time entertaining. Choose from a buffet for 12, a brunch for four, or a holiday menu for eight. Each has a preparation countdown to help simplify getting the meal together. What's more, many of the recipes in this book have make-ahead suggestions. And we've noted the super-fast ones that take 30 minutes or less.

Whether you want a single recipe or a whole meal, *Brunches and Breakfasts* has just what you need to help juggle a delicious morning meal into your family's busy schedule.

Pick-a-Filling Oven Omelet
(see recipe, page 16)
People-Pleasing Rolls
(see recipe, page 42)
Cranberry juice cocktail

Menu

Brunch for a Bunch

Feed 12 hungry people with this midmorning feast. To keep the day of the brunch as hassle-free as possible, do most of the food preparation the day before. Then at mealtime, set the food on a buffet table for simple, help-yourself service. Weather permitting, the deck, porch, or patio makes an ideal place for brunch.

Vegetable-Barley Salad
(see recipe, page 11)

Brunch Loaf
(see recipe, page 8)

Creamy Ham 'n' Egg Bake
(see recipe, page 9)

MENU

Creamy Ham 'n' Egg Bake

Cranberry-Sauced Turkey

Vegetable-Barley Salad *or*

Apricot-Glazed Fruit Salad

Brunch Loaf

Apple Fizz

Coffee *or* Tea

Apple Fizz
(see recipe, page 11)

Cranberry-Sauced Turkey
(see recipe, page 10)

Brunch for a Bunch

MENU

Creamy Ham 'n' Egg Bake
Cranberry-Sauced Turkey
Vegetable-Barley Salad
  or
Apricot-Glazed Fruit Salad
Brunch Loaf
Apple Fizz
Coffee *or* Tea

MENU COUNTDOWN

Up to 1 Month Ahead:
Bake Brunch Loaf; cool, wrap, and freeze.
1 Day Ahead:
Prepare Creamy Ham 'n' Egg Bake; cover and chill. Stir together sauce for the Cranberry-Sauced Turkey and arrange sliced turkey in the baking dish; cover and chill sauce and meat separately. Prepare either the Vegetable-Barley Salad or Apricot-Glazed Fruit Salad; cover and chill. Thaw the juice concentrate in the refrigerator and chill the carbonated water for Apple Fizz.
Several Hours Ahead:
Thaw wrapped Brunch Loaf.

55 Minutes Ahead:
Preheat the oven.
45 Minutes Ahead:
Place Egg Bake in oven.
30 Minutes Ahead:
Place turkey in oven with eggs. Stir the eggs.
15 Minutes Ahead:
Wash lettuce, if using, and place salad in serving bowl. Slice the Brunch Loaf and arrange on a serving plate. Prepare coffee or tea and heat the cranberry mixture.
Just Before Serving:
Combine the Fizz ingredients. Remove turkey from the oven and arrange on a serving platter. Spoon some of the cranberry mixture over turkey; pour remaining sauce into a serving bowl.

Brunch Loaf

Pictured on pages 6 and 7.

1	**cup all-purpose flour**
1	**cup whole wheat flour**
⅔	**cup packed brown sugar**
¼	**cup whole bran cereal**
1	**teaspoon baking soda**
½	**teaspoon ground cinnamon**

● In a medium mixing bowl combine all-purpose flour, whole wheat flour, sugar, bran cereal, baking soda, cinnamon, and ¼ teaspoon *salt*. Make a well in the center of the dry ingredients.

1	**beaten egg**
1	**8-ounce carton vanilla yogurt**
¼	**cup milk**
¼	**cup cooking oil**
½	**cup raisins**

● In a small mixing bowl combine egg, yogurt, milk, and oil. Add yogurt mixture all at once to dry ingredients. Stir just till moistened. *Do not overmix.* Fold in raisins. Pour batter into one greased 8x4x2-inch loaf pan or two greased 7½x3½x2-inch loaf pans.

Bake in a 350° oven till a toothpick inserted near the center comes out clean. Allow about 55 minutes for large loaf or about 35 minutes for small loaves. Cool in pan for 10 minutes. Remove from pan; cool. Makes 14 servings.

Nutrition information per serving: 174 calories, 4 g protein, 30 g carbohydrate, 5 g fat, 21 mg cholesterol, 150 mg sodium, 174 mg potassium.

Make the loaf or loaves ahead and freeze as suggested in the menu countdown. Or, bake the bread the day before and store the wrapped loaf overnight in the refrigerator. Serve whole slices cut from small loaves. Or, halve the slices from the larger loaf.

Creamy Ham 'n' Egg Bake

Pictured on pages 6 and 7.

10 eggs ¼ teaspoon salt 2 tablespoons margarine *or* butter	● In a bowl beat eggs and salt together. In a 10-inch skillet melt margarine or butter over medium heat. Pour in egg mixture. Cook, without stirring, till mixture begins to set on the bottom and around the edges. Using a large spoon or spatula, lift and fold partially cooked eggs so uncooked portion flows underneath. Continue cooking over medium heat about 4 minutes total or till eggs are cooked throughout but are still glossy and moist. Immediately remove eggs from heat; set aside.
3 tablespoons margarine *or* butter 3 tablespoons all-purpose flour ¼ teaspoon pepper 1¾ cups milk 6 ounces process Gruyère or Swiss cheese, cut up (1½ cups) 2 teaspoons prepared mustard	● For sauce, in a 4-quart Dutch oven melt margarine or butter. Stir in flour and pepper. Add milk all at once. Cook and stir till mixture is thickened and bubbly. Add cheese and mustard, stirring till cheese melts.
2 16-ounce packages loose-pack frozen broccoli, corn, and peppers, thawed and well-drained 6 ounces fully cooked ham, cut into bite-size strips (about 1 cup)	● Stir in vegetables and ham, then gently fold in eggs. Turn mixture into a 13x9x2-inch baking dish. Cover and chill for up to 24 hours.
2 ounces process Gruyère *or* Swiss cheese, shredded (½ cup)	● Before serving, cover and bake in a 350° oven for 45 minutes or till heated through, gently stirring after 15 minutes. After baking, gently stir. Sprinkle with cheese. Makes 12 servings.

Nutrition information per serving: 258 calories, 17 g protein, 12 g carbohydrate, 16 g fat, 257 mg cholesterol, 417 mg sodium, 318 mg potassium.

As you're preparing the menu, give the egg mixture a gentle stir when you start heating the turkey. Stirring helps the ingredients heat more evenly.

Apricot-Glazed Fruit Salad

SUPER FAST

Total Time: 25 minutes

1	21-ounce can apricot pie filling
½	cup orange juice
1	to 2 tablespoons lemon juice

● In a very large mixing bowl combine pie filling, orange juice, and lemon juice.

The tasty glaze starts with a can of pie filling. What could be simpler?

4	medium peaches *or* nectarines, peeled, pitted, and sliced (2 cups), *or* 2 cups frozen sliced peaches
2	cups cubed cantaloupe *or* honeydew melon
2	cups seedless red *or* green grapes, halved
2	cups coarsely chopped apples
½	cup toasted flaked coconut

● Stir in the peaches or nectarines, cantaloupe or honeydew melon, red or green grapes, apples, and coconut. Cover and chill in the refrigerator for 2 to 24 hours. Makes 12 servings.

Nutrition information per serving: 156 calories, 1 g protein, 37 g carbohydrate, 1 g fat, 0 mg cholesterol, 15 mg sodium, 244 mg potassium.

Cranberry-Sauced Turkey

Pictured on pages 6 and 7.

1	16-ounce can whole cranberry sauce
½	cup catsup
¼	cup orange marmalade
2	tablespoons orange juice
1	tablespoon dried minced onion

● In a mixing bowl combine cranberry sauce, catsup, orange marmalade, orange juice, and onion. Cover and chill in the refrigerator for up to 24 hours.

Prepackaged, cooked turkey breast is ideal for this recipe. Ask your butcher to slice it for you. Or, purchase turkey breast slices from the deli. A third option is to chill leftover turkey breast, then slice it.

| 2 | to 2½ pounds sliced fully cooked turkey breast, cut ¼ inch thick |

● Arrange turkey slices in a 12x7½x2-inch baking dish. Cover with foil; chill in the refrigerator for up to 24 hours. (Chill sauce and turkey separately.)

● Before serving, bake the turkey, covered, in a 350° oven for 25 to 30 minutes or till heated through.
  Meanwhile, in a medium saucepan heat the cranberry mixture till hot. To serve, use a slotted spatula to transfer turkey to a warm serving platter. Spoon some of the sauce over the turkey slices on the platter. Serve remaining sauce in a bowl. Makes 12 servings.

Nutrition information per serving: 192 calories, 23 g protein, 23 g carbohydrate, 1 g fat, 63 mg cholesterol, 171 mg sodium, 285 mg potassium.

MICROWAVE TIMING: Before serving, arrange turkey in a microwave-safe baking dish. Cover dish with waxed paper. Micro-cook on 70% power (medium-high) for 9 to 12 minutes or till heated through, rearranging pieces twice. Keep warm.
  Micro-cook sauce in a microwave-safe 4-cup measure, uncovered, on 100% power (high) for 5 to 7 minutes or till bubbly; stir once.

Vegetable-Barley Salad

Pictured on pages 6 and 7.

4 cups water 1½ cups quick-cooking barley 1 teaspoon instant chicken 　　bouillon granules	● In a large saucepan bring water to boiling. Add barley and bouillon granules. Return to boiling; reduce heat. Simmer, covered, for 10 to 12 minutes or till barley is tender. Drain and rinse with cold water. Drain well.
1 medium cucumber, 　　chopped (1½ cups) 1 small red *or* green sweet 　　pepper, cut into bite- 　　size strips ¼ cup sliced green onion ¼ cup snipped parsley 1 tablespoon snipped fresh 　　mint *or* 1 teaspoon 　　dried mint leaves, 　　crushed	● In a large mixing bowl stir together drained barley, cucumber, pepper, green onion, parsley, and mint.
½ cup salad oil ½ cup lemon juice 1 tablespoon sugar ¾ teaspoon salt ½ teaspoon pepper 　　Lettuce leaves 　　Fresh mint sprigs 　　(optional)	● For salad dressing, in a screw-top jar combine oil, lemon juice, sugar, salt, and pepper. Cover and shake well. Pour over barley mixture; toss to coat. Cover; chill in the refrigerator for up to 24 hours. 　To serve, line a salad bowl with lettuce leaves. Spoon the barley mixture into the bowl. Garnish with fresh mint, if desired. Makes 12 servings.

Guests will love this delicious barley salad. The garden-fresh vegetables make it look and taste terrific.

Nutrition information per serving: 181 calories, 2 g protein, 23 g carbohydrate, 9 g fat, 0 mg cholesterol, 159 mg sodium, 115 mg potassium.

Total Time: 10 minutes

Apple Fizz

Pictured on pages 6 and 7.

3 6-ounce cans frozen apple 　　juice concentrate, 　　thawed 2 1-liter bottles carbonated 　　water, chilled 　　Ice cubes	● In a large bowl combine thawed apple juice concentrate and carbonated water. Stir gently to mix. If desired, pour into a pitcher for serving. Serve over ice. Makes 12 (7-ounce) servings.

To keep the fizz fizzy, stir the beverage *gently* once the carbonated water is added. Stirring too much can cause some of the bubbles to escape.

Nutrition information per serving: 88 calories, 0 g protein, 22 g carbohydrate, 0 g fat, 0 mg cholesterol, 13 mg sodium, 239 mg potassium.

Shortcut Eggs Benedict

2 **English muffins, split and toasted** 8 **thin slices Canadian-style bacon (about 4 ounces total)**	● In an 8x8x2-inch baking dish arrange toasted muffins, cut side up. Place *2* bacon slices on *each* muffin half.	**This easy-to-fix version of the classic dish skips the poached eggs and uses scrambled eggs and a packaged sauce mix.**

This easy-to-fix version of the classic dish skips the poached eggs and uses scrambled eggs and a packaged sauce mix.

It's also easy to increase the recipe to make 8 servings. Just double all ingredients, *except* use only 1 tablespoon margarine and a sauce mix that makes 1½ cups. Cook eggs for 3 to 4 minutes or till cooked throughout. Assemble the stacks in a 13x9x2-inch baking dish.

---

4 **eggs**
2 **tablespoons milk**
Dash pepper
1 **tablespoon margarine *or* butter**

● In a bowl beat together eggs, milk, and pepper. In a skillet melt margarine or butter over medium heat. Pour in egg mixture. Cook without stirring, till mixture begins to set on the bottom and around the edges. Using a large spoon or spatula, lift and fold partially cooked eggs so uncooked portion flows underneath. Continue cooking over medium heat about 3 minutes total or till eggs are cooked throughout but are still glossy and moist. Immediately remove eggs from heat.

Spoon eggs atop *each* muffin stack, dividing evenly.

---

1 **envelope hollandaise sauce mix (makes about ⅔ cup sauce)**
1 **teaspoon lemon juice**

● Prepare sauce mix according to package directions. Stir in lemon juice. Spoon sauce over muffin stacks.

½ **cup soft bread crumbs (about ½ slice)**
2 **teaspoons snipped chives *or* parsley**
2 **teaspoons margarine *or* butter, melted**
Tomato wedges (optional)

● For crumb topping, combine crumbs, chives or parsley, and margarine or butter; sprinkle over muffin stacks. Bake, uncovered, in a 350° oven about 15 minutes or till heated through. Transfer to a platter or individual plates; spoon any sauce in dish over eggs. If desired, garnish with tomato wedges. Serves 4.

Make-ahead directions: Prepare muffins and stack Canadian-style bacon and *eggs* atop muffins in baking dish up to 24 hours ahead. Prepare crumb topping. Cover and chill main dish and crumbs separately.

To serve, prepare sauce and spoon over muffin stacks. Sprinkle with crumbs. Bake, uncovered, in a 350° oven about 20 minutes or till heated through.

Nutrition information per serving: 292 calories, 18 g protein, 24 g carbohydrate, 14 g fat, 292 mg cholesterol, 756 mg sodium, 222 mg potassium.

Omelet Pizza

1 tablespoon cornmeal
1 6-ounce package pizza
   crust mix

● Grease a 12-inch pizza pan; sprinkle with cornmeal.

   Prepare pizza crust according to package directions. Spread dough in prepared pan, forming the edges at least as high as the sides of the pan, about ¾ inch. Bake in a 400° oven for 10 minutes or till edges are light brown.

7 eggs
⅓ cup milk
¼ teaspoon salt
⅛ teaspoon pepper

● In a mixing bowl combine eggs, milk, salt, and pepper. Using a fork, beat till combined but not frothy. Leaving crust on oven rack, carefully pour egg mixture into the baked crust. Bake in a 400° oven for 10 to 12 minutes or till egg mixture is almost set.

3 tablespoons margarine *or*
   butter
4 tablespoons all-purpose
   flour
½ teaspoon prepared
   mustard
1⅔ cups milk
½ cup dairy sour cream
8 ounces fully cooked
   smoked sausage links,
   halved lengthwise and
   sliced
1 12-ounce can whole kernel
   corn with sweet
   peppers, drained

● Meanwhile, for sauce, in a medium saucepan melt margarine or butter. Stir in *3 tablespoons* of the flour and mustard. Add milk all at once. Cook and stir till thickened and bubbly.

   In a small mixing bowl combine remaining flour and sour cream. Gradually stir *½ cup* of the hot mixture into sour cream mixture; return all to saucepan. Cook and stir till bubbly. Stir in sausage and drained corn. Cook and stir till sauce is heated through.

   Remove pizza from oven and cut into 6 wedges. Serve wedges topped with the sausage-corn sauce. Serves 6.

Nutrition information per serving: 457 calories, 19 g protein, 26 g carbohydrate, 31 g fat, 362 mg cholesterol, 921 mg sodium, 380 mg potassium.

This pizza's different from any you've had before. Instead of the usual pizza toppings, it's covered with a delicious breakfast-style sausage and corn combo. If you like, prepare the sauce the day before. Then, reheat it just before the freshly baked pizza comes out of the oven.

Poached Eggs In Tomato Sauce

SUPER FAST

Total Time: 25 minutes

1	**14½-ounce can stewed tomatoes**
1	**8-ounce can tomato sauce**
1	**clove garlic, minced**
1	**bay leaf**
⅛	**teaspoon pepper**

● Cut up any large pieces of tomato. In a 10-inch skillet combine stewed tomatoes, tomato sauce, garlic, bay leaf, and pepper. Bring to boiling. Reduce heat and simmer, covered, for 5 minutes. Discard bay leaf.

1	**cup frozen peas**
4	**eggs**
4	**ounces fully cooked smoked sausage links, halved lengthwise and sliced, *or* fully cooked ham, cut into matchstick-size strips**

● Stir in peas. Break *1* egg into a small dish and carefully slide into the simmering tomato mixture (see photo, below). Repeat with remaining eggs, allowing each egg an equal amount of space. Arrange sausage slices or ham strips around eggs.

4	**corn muffins, halved *or* sliced**

● Cover; simmer over low heat about 5 minutes or till eggs reach desired doneness. Serve eggs and sauce over muffin halves or slices. Makes 4 servings.

Nutrition information per serving: 374 calories, 16 g protein, 36 g carbohydrate, 19 g fat, 316 mg cholesterol, 1,176 mg sodium, 687 mg potassium.

Save time by using frozen corn muffins for this recipe. There are two kinds available. Prepare the flat version in the toaster according to package directions. Or, thaw regular corn muffins and halve or slice them.

Break one egg at a time into a small dish. Then, holding the lip of the dish as close to the sauce as possible, carefully slide the egg into the simmering mixture. Be careful not to break the yolks as you slip them into the skillet. Space the eggs evenly in the sauce.

Pick-a-Filling Oven Omelet

SUPER FAST

Total Time: 30 minutes

Ham-Raisin Filling *or*
  Pear-Cheese Filling
2 tablespoons margarine *or*
  butter

● Prepare desired filling; set aside. Place margarine or butter in a 15x10x1-inch baking pan. Place the pan in a 400° oven about 2 minutes to melt margarine.

12 eggs
¼ cup water
½ teaspoon salt
⅛ teaspoon pepper

● In a mixing bowl combine eggs, water, salt, and pepper. Using a fork or a rotary beater, beat till combined but not frothy.

  Tilt hot margarine or butter in the pan to thoroughly coat pan. Place the pan on oven rack. Carefully pour egg mixture into the pan. Bake in a 400° oven about 7 minutes or till eggs are set but still have a glossy surface.

Orange slices (optional)
Celery leaves *or* parsley
  sprigs (optional)

● Meanwhile, reheat desired filling. Cut omelet into 6 squares measuring 5x5 inches. Remove each omelet square using a large spatula. Invert omelet squares onto warm serving plates. Spoon some filling on half of each omelet; fold other half over filling, forming a triangle or a rectangle. Top as directed in filling recipe. If desired, garnish with orange slices and celery leaves. Serves 6.

Nutrition information per serving (without filling): 193 calories, 12 g protein, 1 g carbohydrate, 15 g fat, 549 mg cholesterol, 364 mg sodium, 133 mg potassium.

Ham-Raisin Filling: Cut one 6-ounce package of sliced fully cooked *ham* into matchstick-like strips. Peel, core, and chop 1 large *apple* (1⅓ cups). Set ham and apple aside. In a medium saucepan stir together 1⅓ cups *apple juice,* 2 tablespoons *cornstarch,* and ¼ teaspoon ground *cinnamon.* Stir in apple and ¼ cup *raisins.* Cook and stir till mixture is thickened and bubbly. Stir in ham. Cook and stir about 2 minutes or till heated through. Spoon filling onto omelets. Fold omelets. Sprinkle tops with ¼ cup sliced toasted *almonds.* Makes 6 servings.

Nutrition information per serving: 134 calories, 7 g protein, 19 g carbohydrate, 4 g fat, 15 mg cholesterol, 344 mg sodium, 251 mg potassium.

Pear-Cheese Filling: In a mixing bowl combine ⅓ cup *soft-style cream cheese* and 3 tablespoons shredded *cheddar cheese or* crumbled *blue cheese;* set aside. Peel, core, and thinly slice 3 *pears or apples.* In a large skillet cook fruit, covered, over medium-low heat in 1 tablespoon *margarine or butter* about 5 minutes or till tender. Add 1 tablespoon *sugar.* Cook and stir about 1 minute or till sugar is dissolved. Spoon warm fruit filling onto omelets. Divide cheese mixture atop fruit. Fold omelets. Sprinkle omelet tops with ¼ cup chopped *pecans.* Makes 6 servings.

Nutrition information per serving: 160 calories, 2 g protein, 14 g carbohydrate, 11 g fat, 4 mg cholesterol, 79 mg sodium, 127 mg potassium.

Curried Eggs Over Chow Mein Noodles

½ cup chopped green pepper
¼ cup chopped onion
1 to 2 teaspoons curry powder
2 tablespoons margarine *or* butter
3 tablespoons all-purpose flour
2 teaspoons instant chicken bouillon granules
⅛ teaspoon pepper
2¼ cups milk

● In a large saucepan cook green pepper, onion, and curry powder in margarine or butter till vegetables are tender but not brown. Stir in flour, bouillon granules, and pepper. Add milk all at once. Cook and stir till mixture is thickened and bubbly. Cook and stir for 1 minute more.

Creamy and crunchy—this recipe is both. A creamy curry sauce is served over crunchy chow mein noodles.

Cook the eggs ahead of time and you'll have a head start on brunch.

6 hard-cooked eggs
6 slices bacon, crisp-cooked, drained, and crumbled
1 3-ounce can chow mein noodles *or* 6 ounces spaghetti, cooked
2 tablespoons snipped parsley

● Slice eggs. Fold eggs and bacon into sauce; heat through. Serve over chow mein noodles or hot spaghetti. Sprinkle with parsley. Serve with apple wedges, if desired. Makes 4 servings.

Nutrition information per serving: 440 calories, 21 g protein, 27 g carbohydrate, 28 g fat, 435 mg cholesterol, 818 mg sodium, 463 mg potassium.

All About Eggs . . .

Have questions about eggs? Here are the answers to a few common egg queries.
● Is there a difference between brown and white eggs? There's no difference in quality or nutritional value between the two. Shell color depends on the breed of the hen.
● What's the best way to hard-cook eggs? Place eggs in a saucepan. Add enough cold water to cover the eggs. Bring to boiling over high heat. Reduce heat so water is just below simmering. Cover and cook 15 minutes. Pour off the water, then fill the saucepan with cold water and let stand 2 minutes. To quickly cool the eggs, add a few ice cubes to the water. Drain.
● Is there a substitute for whole eggs? Egg whites can be substituted for whole eggs in certain recipes. Check the notes following several of the recipes in this book. Commercial egg substitute products are also available; check the label for recipe suggestions.
● What size eggs should I use? For the recipes in this book, our Test Kitchen recommends using large eggs.

Carrot and Bacon Quiche

1 **9-inch folded refrigerated unbaked piecrust**
4 **slices bacon, crisp-cooked, drained, and crumbled, *or* 2 tablespoons cooked bacon pieces**

● Let piecrust stand at room temperature according to package directions. Meanwhile, prepare foil "shell" (see photo, top right).
   Prepare piecrust according to package directions, *except* do not prick the crust. Place the foil "shell" atop the crust.
   Bake in a 450° oven for 5 minutes. Carefully remove foil. Bake for 5 minutes more. Remove from oven. Reduce oven temperature to 325°. Place bacon pieces in piecrust; set aside.

Foil helps keep an unpricked piecrust from puffing and shrinking.
   To make the foil "shell," press a double thickness of heavy-duty foil into a 9-inch pie plate, molding it to the shape of the pie plate, as shown. Remove foil, keeping its shape. Place atop unbaked piecrust the first few minutes of baking.

½ **cup finely shredded carrot**
¼ **cup chopped green onion**

● In a small saucepan cook carrot and green onion in a small amount of water about 4 minutes or till tender. Drain, pressing out excess liquid with the back of a spoon; set vegetables aside.

3 **beaten eggs**
1½ **cups milk**
¼ **teaspoon salt**
   Dash ground nutmeg
1½ **cups shredded Swiss cheese (6 ounces)**
1 **tablespoon all-purpose flour**

● In a mixing bowl stir together eggs, milk, salt, and nutmeg. Add carrot and onion; set aside. Toss together cheese and flour; sprinkle over bacon in piecrust. Place piecrust with bacon and cheese mixture on oven rack; carefully pour in egg-vegetable mixture.
   Bake in the 325° oven for 40 to 45 minutes or till done (see photo, bottom right). Let stand 10 minutes before cutting into wedges. Makes 6 servings.

Nutrition information per serving: 374 calories, 16 g protein, 22 g carbohydrate, 24 g fat, 173 mg cholesterol, 447 mg sodium, 240 mg potassium.

Test a quiche for doneness by inserting a knife near the center of the pie. The knife should come out clean, as shown. If some of the egg mixture remains on the knife, bake a few minutes longer.

Egg-Enchilada Skillet

Total Time: 15 minutes

8 eggs
⅛ teaspoon garlic powder
1 tablespoon margarine *or* butter

● In a bowl beat together eggs and garlic powder. In a 10-inch skillet melt margarine or butter over medium heat. Pour in egg mixture. Cook, without stirring, till mixture begins to set on the bottom and around the edges. Using a large spoon or spatula, lift and fold partially cooked eggs so uncooked portion flows underneath. Continue cooking over medium heat for 2 to 3 minutes or till eggs are cooked throughout but are still glossy and moist.

2 cups tortilla chips
1 10-ounce can enchilada sauce
1 2¼-ounce can sliced pitted ripe olives, drained (½ cup)
½ cup shredded Monterey Jack cheese (2 ounces)
½ cup dairy sour cream
1 green onion, sliced

● Add tortilla chips, enchilada sauce, and olives. Stir gently to combine. Sprinkle with cheese; cover and cook over low heat about 5 minutes or till heated through. Serve immediately dolloped with sour cream and sprinkled with green onion. Makes 4 or 5 servings.

Nutrition information per serving: 415 calories, 18 g protein, 17 g carbohydrate, 30 g fat, 576 mg cholesterol, 984 mg sodium, 371 mg potassium.

Some like it hot; others like it even hotter. The mild enchilada sauce gives this skillet dish plenty of spiciness. But if you enjoy extra spicy foods, use hot enchilada sauce *or* Monterey Jack cheese with jalapeño peppers.

No-Chop Spinach and Potato Pie

4 beaten eggs
1 tablespoon milk
½ teaspoon garlic salt
⅛ teaspoon pepper

● In a mixing bowl combine eggs, milk, garlic salt, and pepper.

1½ cups loose-pack frozen hash brown potatoes with onions and peppers
1 10-ounce package frozen chopped spinach, thawed and well drained
½ cup shredded Swiss cheese (2 ounces)

● Add potatoes, spinach, and cheese to egg mixture in bowl. Pour into a well-greased 8-inch skillet.
 Cook, covered, over medium heat for 10 to 12 minutes or till center is soft-set and bottom is golden. Remove from heat; let stand, covered, for 5 minutes. Cut into wedges. Makes 3 servings.

Nutrition information per serving: 366 calories, 18 g protein, 26 g carbohydrate, 22 g fat, 384 mg cholesterol, 536 mg sodium, 797 mg potassium.

The spinach in this pie is a very good source of vitamin A. In fact, each serving contributes more than 100% of the U.S. RDA for vitamin A.

Cheese and Broccoli Soufflé

¼ cup margarine *or* butter
¼ cup all-purpose flour
⅛ teaspoon salt
Dash ground red pepper
Dash dry mustard
1 cup milk
1 cup finely chopped, cooked broccoli
½ cup finely shredded cheddar cheese *or* crumbled blue cheese (2 ounces)

● Attach a buttered foil collar to a 1½-quart soufflé dish (see photo, below).

In a medium saucepan melt margarine or butter over medium-high heat. Stir in flour, salt, pepper, and mustard. Add milk all at once. Cook and stir till thickened and bubbly. Remove from heat. Add cooked broccoli and cheese to milk mixture, stirring till cheese melts.

Soufflés are best just as they come from the oven. So, be sure to have everyone seated and ready to enjoy this cloudlike delight.

To serve, use two forks held back to back to gently break the top crust into serving-size portions. Then, spoon the delicate portions onto plates.

4 eggs
½ teaspoon cream of tartar

● Separate eggs. In a mixing bowl beat egg yolks with a fork till combined. Gradually add the broccoli mixture, stirring constantly; set aside.

In a large bowl beat egg whites and cream of tartar with an electric mixer on high speed till stiff peaks form (tips stand straight). Gently fold about *1 cup* of the beaten egg whites into vegetable mixture to lighten it. Gradually pour vegetable mixture over remaining beaten egg whites, folding to combine. Pour egg mixture into the *ungreased* soufflé dish.

Bake in a 350° oven for 35 to 40 minutes or till a knife inserted near the center comes out clean. Gently peel off the foil. Serve the soufflé immediately. Makes 4 servings.

Nutrition information per serving: 309 calories, 14 g protein, 12 g carbohydrate, 23 g fat, 295 mg cholesterol, 394 mg sodium, 251 mg potassium.

For the foil collar on a soufflé dish, measure enough foil to go around the dish plus a 2- to 3-inch overlap. Fold the foil into thirds lengthwise. Lightly butter one side of the foil. With the buttered side in, position the foil around the soufflé dish, letting the foil extend 2 inches above the top of the dish. Fasten the foil with masking tape.

Salmon Skillet Puff

2 tablespoons sliced green onion 1 tablespoon margarine *or* butter 2 teaspoons all-purpose flour ⅛ teaspoon salt ½ cup milk	● Preheat the oven to 325°. Meanwhile, in a small saucepan cook onion in margarine or butter till tender but not brown. Stir in flour and salt. Add milk all at once. Cook and stir till mixture is thickened and bubbly. Set aside.
4 eggs 1 6¾-ounce can skinless, boneless salmon, drained and flaked 2 tablespoons diced pimiento	● Separate eggs. In a small mixing bowl beat egg yolks. Gradually stir in the thickened mixture. In a large bowl beat egg whites till stiff peaks form (tips stand straight). Gradually pour thickened yolk mixture over beaten egg whites, gently folding to combine. Fold in salmon and pimiento.
2 tablespoons margarine *or* butter	● In a 10-inch ovenproof skillet heat margarine or butter till a drop of water sizzles. Pour in egg mixture, mounding it higher at sides. Cook, uncovered, over low heat for 5 minutes or till puffed and set on edges. Immediately place skillet in a 325° oven. Bake for 10 to 12 minutes or till a knife inserted near the center comes out clean.
¼ cup plain yogurt ¼ cup mayonnaise *or* salad dressing ¼ teaspoon finely shredded lemon peel ¼ teaspoon dried dillweed	● For sauce, in a bowl stir together yogurt, mayonnaise or salad dressing, lemon peel, and dillweed. Serve sauce over each serving of the puff. Serves 4. Nutrition information per serving: 359 calories, 16 g protein, 5 g carbohydrate, 30 g fat, 300 mg cholesterol, 361 mg sodium, 329 mg potassium.

This salmon main dish is similar to a soufflé, but it's made in a skillet. It starts on the range top then finishes cooking in the oven.

Potato-Broccoli Frittata

2 cups frozen *or* fresh
   chopped broccoli
1 potato, sliced
2 tablespoons olive oil *or*
   cooking oil
½ cup chopped onion
¼ cup finely chopped red *or*
   green sweet pepper
1 small clove garlic, minced

● Thaw broccoli, if frozen. In a 10-inch skillet cook potato slices, uncovered, in hot oil for 5 minutes or till just tender, turning occasionally. Add onion, pepper, and garlic. Cook till onion is tender. Add broccoli; reduce heat. Cook, covered, for 5 minutes more.

Take your choice—peel the potato or leave the skin on for this egg dish. You'll save a little time and effort using the unpeeled potato.

6 eggs
½ cup grated Parmesan
   cheese
¼ cup water
½ teaspoon dried basil,
   crushed
¼ teaspoon salt
⅛ teaspoon pepper

● Beat together eggs, cheese, water, basil, salt, and pepper. Pour over vegetables in skillet. Cook over medium-low heat for 5 to 6 minutes. As eggs set, run a spatula around the edge of skillet, lifting egg mixture to allow uncooked portion to flow underneath. Continue cooking and lifting edge till mixture is almost set. (The surface will be moist.)

1 tablespoon grated
   Parmesan cheese

● Remove skillet from heat. Cover and let stand for 3 to 4 minutes or till top is set. Sprinkle with cheese. Cut into wedges; serve from the skillet. Serves 4.

Nutrition information per serving: 298 calories, 18 g protein, 13 g carbohydrate, 20 g fat, 423 mg cholesterol, 516 mg sodium, 498 mg potassium.

Cook the egg mixture over medium-low heat. If the temperature is too hot, the egg mixture will overcook and become tough. As the eggs begin to set, run a wide spatula around the edge of the skillet and lift the eggs. Lifting allows the uncooked portion to flow underneath and cook.

Garden Salad Puffy Omelet

5 eggs
3 tablespoons water

● Preheat the oven to 325°. Meanwhile, separate eggs. In a mixing bowl beat egg yolks with a fork or rotary beater.

In a large bowl beat egg whites till frothy. Add water. Continue beating till stiff peaks form (tips stand straight). Gradually pour yolk mixture over beaten egg whites, gently folding to combine.

1 tablespoon margarine *or* butter

● In a 10-inch ovenproof skillet heat margarine or butter till a drop of water sizzles. Pour in egg mixture, mounding it slightly higher at the sides. Cook, uncovered, over low heat for 8 to 10 minutes or till puffed, set, and golden brown on the bottom.

Immediately place skillet in a 325° oven. Bake for 8 to 10 minutes or till a knife inserted near the center comes out clean. Loosen sides of the omelet with a spatula. Invert omelet onto a warm plate.

¾ cup shredded Monterey Jack cheese (3 ounces)
½ cup alfalfa sprouts
2 tablespoons chopped green pepper
2 tablespoons sunflower nuts
4 cherry tomatoes, sliced Milk
3 tablespoons creamy buttermilk salad dressing

● For cheese-vegetable topping, sprinkle omelet with cheese, then sprouts, green pepper, sunflower nuts, and tomatoes. Stir about 1 teaspoon milk into dressing; drizzle over top. Cut into wedges to serve. Makes 4 servings.

Nutrition information per serving: 269 calories, 14 g protein, 3 g carbohydrate, 22 g fat, 363 mg cholesterol, 331 mg sodium, 160 mg potassium.

Fruit-Topped Puffy Omelet: Prepare omelet as directed above, *except* omit cheese-vegetable topping. Instead, top with 1½ cups *blueberries, raspberries, or* sliced *strawberries.* In a mixing bowl beat together one 3-ounce package *cream cheese,* softened; 4 teaspoons *powdered sugar;* and ¼ teaspoon *vanilla.* Beat in 2 to 3 tablespoons *milk* to make of drizzling consistency. Drizzle over fruit.

Nutrition information per serving: 243 calories, 10 g protein, 12 g carbohydrate, 18 g fat, 368 mg cholesterol, 192 mg sodium, 175 mg potassium.

This omelet features either savory or sweet toppings. For a savory omelet, add the vegetables, Monterey Jack cheese, and salad dressing. For the sweet version, try fresh berries with a cream cheese drizzle.

Turkey and Vegetable Wedges

2 cups packaged biscuit mix
½ teaspoon paprika
2 beaten eggs*
1 tablespoon cooking oil*

● In a mixing bowl stir together biscuit mix and paprika. Add eggs and oil; stir till combined. Shape mixture into a ball.

On a lightly floured surface knead dough a few times till smooth. Roll dough into a 14-inch circle. Place on a greased 12-inch pizza pan, building up edges by folding under excess dough. Bake in a 375° oven about 12 minutes. Cool slightly.

Here's an out-of-the-ordinary brunch dish that's full of color and tastes delicious. Cut it into wedges and serve it just like a pizza.

½ cup mayonnaise *or* salad dressing*
½ cup dairy sour cream*
1 tablespoon snipped parsley
½ teaspoon dried dillweed
Dash pepper
2 cups coarsely chopped cooked turkey
2 tablespoons finely chopped onion

● In a mixing bowl stir together mayonnaise or salad dressing, sour cream, parsley, dillweed, and pepper. Stir in turkey and onion. Spread mixture evenly over crust. Bake in the 375° oven for 15 minutes.

2 medium tomatoes, seeded and chopped
1 medium green pepper, cut into thin strips
1 cup shredded cheddar *or* Swiss cheese (4 ounces)*

● Top with tomato, pepper, and cheese. Bake for 5 to 10 minutes more or till heated through and cheese is melted. Serve immediately. Makes 6 servings.

Nutrition information per serving: 553 calories, 25 g protein, 31 g carbohydrate, 37 g fat, 167 mg cholesterol, 794 mg sodium, 363 mg potassium.

Note: To reduce calories, fat, and cholesterol, omit eggs and oil in crust and replace with ⅓ cup *water*. Use *reduced-calorie mayonnaise or salad dressing*, substitute *plain low-fat yogurt* for sour cream, and substitute *mozzarella cheese* for the cheddar or Swiss cheese. (379 calories, 17 g fat, 55 mg cholesterol per serving)

Brunch Turnovers

½ of a 17¼-ounce package (1 sheet) frozen puff pastry

● Let frozen pastry sheet stand at room temperature about 20 minutes or till thawed. Unfold pastry and roll into a 12-inch square.

You can assemble the turnovers up to 24 hours ahead. Just cover and refrigerate them on the baking sheet. To heat, uncover them and bake as described in the recipe.

---

2 tablespoons finely chopped onion
1 tablespoon margarine *or* butter
1 beaten egg
1 cup shredded Swiss cheese (4 ounces)
1 cup finely chopped fully cooked ham (5 ounces)
1 tablespoon snipped parsley
1 teaspoon dried dillweed
Dash garlic powder
Dash pepper

● In a small saucepan cook onion in hot margarine or butter till tender but not brown. For filling, in a medium mixing bowl combine egg, cheese, ham, parsley, dillweed, garlic powder, and pepper. Stir in onion mixture; set aside.

● Cut pastry sheet into quarters. (You should have four 6-inch squares.) Place about *½ cup* of the filling just off center of *each* square. Moisten edges of pastry with water; fold in half diagonally. Seal edges by pressing with tines of a fork or with fingers. Place turnovers on an ungreased baking sheet.

Bake in a 400° oven for 20 to 25 minutes or till golden. Let stand about 10 minutes before serving. Serves 4.

Nutrition information per serving: 336 calories, 19 g protein, 14 g carbohydrate, 23 g fat, 113 mg cholesterol, 700 mg sodium, 174 mg potassium.

Quick-Cooking Meats

Small, thin cuts of meat are perfect for breakfast and brunch because they cook so quickly. Take your choice of any of these:

STEAKS, CHOPS, CUTLETS: To panbroil ½-inch-thick *beef cubed steaks,* ¼-inch-thick *pork chops, or* ¼-inch-thick *veal cutlets,* brush a preheated skillet lightly with *cooking oil* (omit oil for pork chops). Add meat. *Do not cover.* Reduce heat to medium and cook till well done, turning meat over after half of the cooking time.

Allow 5 to 8 minutes for beef cubed steaks, 5 to 7 minutes for pork chops, and 3 to 5 minutes for veal cutlets. (If meat browns too quickly, reduce heat slightly.) Spoon off fat and juices as they accumulate during cooking.

HAM, CANADIAN-STYLE BACON: To panbroil a 1-inch-thick *ham slice* or ¼-inch-thick *Canadian-style bacon* slices, place meat in a cool skillet. *Do not cover.* Turn heat to medium and cook till heated, turning meat over after half of the cooking time.

Allow 16 to 18 minutes for the ham slice and 3 to 5 minutes for the Canadian-style bacon slices. If meat browns too quickly, reduce heat slightly.

BACON: To panbroil *bacon,* place slices in a cool skillet. Cook, uncovered, till bacon is crisp, turning occasionally. Allow 8 to 10 minutes. Drain well.

SAUSAGE: To panbroil ½-inch-thick uncooked *pork sausage patties or* ¾-inch-diameter uncooked *pork sausage links,* place sausage in a cool skillet and cook, uncovered, over medium-low heat till juices run clear. Allow 10 to 12 minutes for patties, turning once, and 10 to 15 minutes for links, turning often. Drain well.

Veal and Asparagus Newburg

1 **pound fresh asparagus spears** *or* **one 10-ounce package frozen asparagus spears**
12 **ounces veal scallopini** *or* **12 ounces veal leg round steak** *or* **veal leg sirloin steak, cut ½ inch thick**
¼ **teaspoon lemon-pepper seasoning**

● Wash fresh asparagus and scrape off scales, if desired. Break off woody bases where spears snap easily. In a large saucepan cook asparagus spears, covered, in a small amount of boiling water for 8 to 10 minutes or till asparagus is crisp-tender. (*Or,* cook frozen asparagus according to package directions.) Drain; keep warm.

Meanwhile, if necessary, cut veal into serving-size pieces; pound veal steak to ¼-inch thickness. Sprinkle veal with lemon-pepper seasoning; set aside.

1 **6½-ounce package frozen lobster Newburg**
1 **tablespoon white wine**

● In a saucepan cook lobster Newburg according to package directions. Remove sauce from pouch and pour into a bowl. Stir in wine; keep warm.

2 **tablespoons margarine** *or* **butter**

● In a 10- or 12-inch skillet melt margarine or butter over medium-high heat. (Add more margarine, as necessary, during cooking.) Cook veal, half at a time, in margarine for 1 to 2 minutes on each side or till brown. Keep veal warm.

8 **lemon wedges (optional)**

● To serve, place veal on 4 individual plates. Top with asparagus spears. Spoon some of the Newburg sauce over each serving. If desired, serve with lemon. Makes 4 servings.

Nutrition information per serving: 357 calories, 28 g protein, 6 g carbohydrate, 24 g fat, 82 mg cholesterol, 375 mg sodium, 594 mg potassium.

Teaming veal with asparagus and lobster makes an elegant entrée. Just add some fresh fruit and warm croissants to round out the menu.

Dill Fillets With Apple Mayonnaise

Total Time: 25 minutes

1 small apple
2 tablespoons walnuts
¼ teaspoon finely shredded orange peel
2 teaspoons orange juice
¼ cup mayonnaise *or* salad dressing
1 teaspoon snipped chives
¼ cup whipping cream

● For apple mixture, core apple. Finely chop apple and nuts. Toss with orange peel and juice. Stir in mayonnaise or salad dressing and chives. Beat whipping cream to soft peaks. Fold into apple mixture. Cover and chill.

The mayonnaise topping is a savory apple-walnut mixture that's great with any of the fish varieties suggested in the recipe.

1 pound skinless flounder, orange roughy, *or* sole fillets
⅓ cup fine dry bread crumbs
2 tablespoons margarine *or* butter, melted
½ teaspoon dried dillweed

● Lightly grease a 10x6x2-inch baking dish. Measure thickness of fish fillets. Place large fillets in a single layer, tucking under any thin edges (see photo, below). (If using thin fillets, stack them so they are an even thickness.)
  In a small mixing bowl combine crumbs, margarine or butter, and dill. Sprinkle mixture evenly over fish.

MICROWAVE TIMING: To cook fish, arrange in a microwave-safe dish; cover with vented microwave-safe clear plastic wrap. Micro-cook on 100% power (high) for 3 minutes. Rotate dish a half-turn and cook, covered, on high for 2 to 4 minutes more or till fish is done.

● Bake, uncovered, in a 450° oven till fish flakes with a fork and crumbs are golden (allow 4 to 6 minutes per ½-inch thickness of fish). Serve with apple mixture. Makes 4 servings.

Nutrition information per serving: 370 calories, 21 g protein, 13 g carbohydrate, 26 g fat, 86 mg cholesterol, 301 mg sodium, 488 mg potassium.

If fish fillets are thick at one end and thin at the other, turn the thin ends under so the fillets become an even thickness. Then, the fish will cook more evenly without overcooking the thinner ends.

Salmon-Tortilla Bake

1 6¾-ounce can skinless, boneless salmon, drained and flaked
1½ cups loose-pack frozen cut broccoli, thawed, drained, and chopped
½ cup sour cream dip with toasted onion
1 2-ounce jar diced pimiento, drained
1½ teaspoons all-purpose flour
    Several dashes bottled hot pepper sauce
4 6-inch flour tortillas

● In a mixing bowl combine salmon, broccoli, sour cream dip, pimiento, flour, and hot pepper sauce. Spoon about ½ *cup* of the mixture at one edge of *each* tortilla; roll up. Arrange tortilla, seam side down, in a greased 8x8x2-inch baking dish. Repeat with remaining tortillas and salmon mixture.

Salmon makes this a great-tasting brunch casserole, but tuna is also a delicious option. Use a 6½-ounce can in place of the salmon.

2 tablespoons margarine *or* butter
2 tablespoons all-purpose flour
¼ teaspoon salt
1¼ cups milk
1 teaspoon Dijon-style mustard
2 tablespoons grated Parmesan cheese
1 tablespoon snipped parsley

● In a small saucepan melt margarine or butter. Stir in flour and salt. Add milk all at once. Cook and stir till thickened and bubbly. Stir in mustard; mix well. Pour over tortillas in baking dish. Sprinkle with Parmesan cheese.
    Bake, covered, in a 350° oven about 35 minutes or till heated through. Sprinkle with parsley. Makes 4 servings.

Nutrition information per serving: 336 calories, 16 g protein, 25 g carbohydrate, 19 g fat, 35 mg cholesterol, 375 mg sodium, 451 mg potassium.

Attention, Microwave Owners!

The microwave timings in this book were tested using countertop microwave ovens with 600 to 700 watts of cooking power. The cooking times are approximate because microwave ovens vary by manufacturer.

Sunrise Whole Wheat Griddle Cakes

Total Time: 30 minutes

Apricot Sauce (optional)
1½ cups all-purpose flour
1½ cups whole wheat flour
1 tablespoon baking powder
1 tablespoon brown sugar
½ teaspoon salt

● If desired, prepare Apricot Sauce; keep warm. In a large mixing bowl combine all-purpose flour, whole wheat flour, baking powder, sugar, and salt.

2 beaten eggs*
2 cups milk*
3 tablespoons cooking oil
½ cup chopped pecans*

● In another mixing bowl combine eggs, milk, and oil. Add all at once to dry ingredients, stirring with a fork till completely moistened. Stir in pecans.

● For *each* pancake, pour about ¼ cup of the batter onto a hot, lightly greased griddle or heavy skillet, making about 18 pancakes. If necessary, spread batter to a 4-inch circle. Cook till pancakes are golden brown, turning to cook other sides when pancakes have bubbly surfaces and slightly dry edges. If desired, serve with Apricot Sauce. Makes 18 pancakes (6 to 8 servings).

Nutrition information per pancake: 139 calories, 4 g protein, 18 g carbohydrate, 6 g fat, 33 mg cholesterol, 132 mg sodium, 112 mg potassium.

*__Note:__ To reduce calories, fat, and cholesterol, substitute 4 stiff-beaten *egg whites* for the 2 whole eggs and fold into batter. Use *skim milk* and substitute *raisins* for the pecans. Omit the Apricot Sauce and serve with applesauce, if desired. (120 calories, 3 g fat, 0 mg cholesterol per pancake)

Apricot Sauce: In a small saucepan stir together one 12-ounce can *apricot nectar* and 4 teaspoons *cornstarch*. Cook and stir over medium heat till thickened and bubbly. Cook and stir for 2 minutes more. Stir in 2 tablespoons *honey,* 1 tablespoon *margarine or butter,* ¼ teaspoon finely shredded *lemon peel,* and 1 tablespoon *lemon juice.* Stir till margarine melts. Makes about 1½ cups.

Nutrition information per tablespoon: 20 calories, 0 g protein, 4 g carbohydrate, 1 g fat, 0 mg cholesterol, 6 mg sodium, 20 mg potassium

Nuts, apricot nectar, and whole grain goodness— that's what goes into this sunrise pancake feast. Add some crispy bacon and you're in business for a hearty breakfast or brunch.

Fruited Buttermilk Oven Pancakes

1½ **cups all-purpose flour**
 2 **tablespoons sugar**
 1 **teaspoon baking soda**
 1 **teaspoon baking powder**
 ¼ **teaspoon salt**

● In a mixing bowl combine flour, sugar, soda, baking powder, and salt.

Skip griddling individual pancakes. How? Bake all four servings together in the oven. The result? Light, cakey, square pancakes.

 1 **beaten egg***
1½ **cups buttermilk**
 3 **tablespoons cooking oil**

● In another mixing bowl combine egg, buttermilk, and cooking oil. Add all at once to dry ingredients. Stir just till mixed but still slightly lumpy.

 ¾ **cup fresh *or* frozen blueberries, rinsed and drained, *or* one 8¼-ounce can crushed pineapple, drained, *or* 1 medium apple, peeled, cored, and coarsely chopped**
 2 **tablespoons sugar**
 ½ **teaspoon ground cinnamon**
    Orange Butter* (optional)
    Maple-flavored syrup (optional)

● Spread batter evenly in a greased and floured 15x10x1-inch baking pan. Sprinkle fruit over top of the batter. Combine sugar and cinnamon; sprinkle evenly over fruit.
  Bake in a 350° oven for 16 to 18 minutes or till top springs back when lightly touched and top is lightly brown around the edges. Cut into 12 square pancakes. Serve with Orange Butter and maple-flavored syrup, if desired. Makes 12 pancakes (4 to 6 servings).

Nutrition information per pancake: 128 calories, 3 g protein, 19 g carbohydrate, 4 g fat, 24 mg cholesterol, 199 mg sodium, 76 mg potassium.

*__Note:__ To reduce calories and cholesterol, substitute 2 slightly beaten *egg whites* for the whole egg. Omit the Orange Butter and serve with syrup, if desired. (124 calories, 4 g fat, 1 mg cholesterol per pancake)

Orange Butter: Soften ½ cup *margarine or butter.* Beat in 1 teaspoon finely shredded *orange peel* and 1 tablespoon *orange juice* till combined. Makes about ½ cup.

Nutrition information per tablespoon: 103 calories, 0 g protein, 0 g carbohydrate, 11 g fat, 0 mg cholesterol, 134 mg sodium, 10 mg potassium.

Overnight Three-Grain Waffles

1¼ cups all-purpose flour 1 cup yellow cornmeal ½ cup oat bran 3 tablespoons sugar 1 package active dry yeast ½ teaspoon salt	● In a large mixing bowl combine flour, cornmeal, bran, sugar, yeast, and salt.

Look for oat bran in the cereal section of your supermarket.

Or, in place of oat bran, you can use rolled oats. Process ⅔ cup rolled oats in a covered blender container or food processor bowl till ground; substitute for the ½ cup oat bran.

2 cups milk* 2 eggs* ⅓ cup cooking oil	● Add milk, eggs, and oil; beat with a rotary beater or an electric mixer for 1 minute on medium speed till thoroughly combined. Cover loosely and let stand for 1 hour at room temperature or for 2 to 24 hours in the refrigerator till mixture is bubbly and slightly thickened.

Praline Sauce* (optional)	● Stir batter. Pour batter into a preheated, lightly greased waffle baker. (Check manufacturer's directions for amount of batter to use.) Close lid quickly; do not open during baking. Bake according to manufacturer's directions. Using a fork, remove the baked waffle from the grid. Keep hot. Repeat with remaining batter. If desired, serve immediately with Praline Sauce. Makes 4 (8-inch) waffles.

Nutrition information per waffle: 606 calories, 17 g protein, 78 g carbohydrate, 26 g fat, 146 mg cholesterol, 365 mg sodium, 415 mg potassium.

*Note: To reduce calories, fat, and cholesterol, use skim milk and substitute 4 egg whites for the whole eggs. Omit the Praline Sauce. If desired, serve with pancake and waffle syrup. (565 calories, 21 g fat, 2 mg cholesterol per waffle)

Praline Sauce: In a small saucepan combine ¾ cup *sugar,* ¾ cup *packed brown sugar,* and ½ cup *light cream.* Cook and stir over medium-high heat till boiling, stirring constantly to dissolve sugars. Boil, uncovered, for 1 minute. Remove from heat. Stir in ⅓ cup coarsely chopped *pecans,* 1 tablespoon *margarine or butter,* and ½ teaspoon *vanilla.* Stir till margarine melts. Makes about 1½ cups sauce.

Nutrition information per tablespoon: 71 calories, 0 g protein, 13 g carbohydrate, 2 g fat, 2 mg cholesterol, 10 mg sodium, 37 mg potassium.

Cheesecake Crepes

1½ **cups milk***
1 **cup all-purpose flour**
2 **eggs***
1 **tablespoon cooking oil***
¼ **teaspoon salt**

● For crepes, in a bowl combine milk, flour, eggs, oil, and salt. Beat with a rotary beater till well mixed. Heat a lightly greased 6-inch skillet. Remove from heat. Spoon in *2 tablespoons* batter; spread batter (see photo, below). Return to heat; brown on one side only. Invert pan over paper towels; remove crepe. Repeat with remaining batter to make 18, greasing skillet occasionally.

1 **beaten egg***
1 **8-ounce package cream**
   cheese*
1 **cup dry cottage cheese**
2 **tablespoons sugar**
1 **teaspoon vanilla**
   Pineapple-Berry Sauce
   (optional) (see recipe,
   opposite page)

● For filling, beat together egg, cheeses, sugar, and vanilla. Spoon *1 rounded tablespoon* in center of unbrowned side of *each* crepe. Fold crepes (see photo, below). Place crepes in a 12x7½x2-inch baking dish. Cover; heat in a 350° oven for 20 minutes or till hot. If desired, serve sauce over crepes. Serves 6.

Nutrition information per serving (without sauce): 342 calories, 16 g protein, 25 g carbohydrate, 20 g fat, 186 mg cholesterol, 271 mg sodium, 203 mg potassium.

***Note:** To reduce calories, fat, and cholesterol in the crepes, use *skim milk,* use 1 whole egg and 1 *egg white* instead of the 2 whole eggs, and omit cooking oil. For the filling, substitute *Neufchâtel cheese* for the cream cheese and use only the *egg white.* (278 calories, 13 g fat, 78 mg cholesterol per serving)

If you like, make and fill the crepes the day before. Then cover and refrigerate them. To serve, allow about 30 minutes to bake the chilled, filled crepes. While the crepes are heating, fix the sauce.

Spread 2 tablespoons crepe batter in skillet by lifting and tilting skillet to swirl batter and coat pan in a thin, even layer.

To fold packets, start with two opposite sides and fold to the center. Then fold in remaining two sides, overlapping edges.

Pineapple-Berry Sauce: Drain one 15¼-ounce can *pineapple tidbits (juice pack),* reserving juice. Set pineapple aside. Add *orange juice* (about ⅔ cup) to pineapple juice to make 1¼ cups liquid. In a medium saucepan combine ¼ cup *sugar* and 2 tablespoons *cornstarch.* Stir in juice mixture. Cook and stir over medium heat till thickened and bubbly; cook and stir 2 minutes more. Gently stir in 1½ cups sliced *strawberries or* whole *raspberries* and pineapple tidbits. Makes 3 cups sauce.

Nutrition information per ½ cup: 116 calories, 1 g protein, 29 g carbohydrate, 0 g fat, 0 mg cholesterol, 2 mg sodium, 246 mg potassium.

Total Time: 30 minutes

Crumb-Coated Oven Toast

3 beaten eggs*
½ cup milk*

● In a shallow mixing bowl or pie plate combine eggs and milk.

8 slices raisin bread
1 cup graham cracker crumbs (14 square crackers)
Strawberry-Rhubarb Sauce (optional)

● Dip one bread slice in egg mixture, coating both sides. Then dip bread into the crumbs, turning to coat the other side. Place coated slice on a greased baking sheet. Repeat with remaining bread and coating.
 Bake in a 450° oven about 6 minutes or till golden brown. Turn slices over and bake for 5 minutes more. If desired, serve with warm Strawberry-Rhubarb Sauce. Makes 4 servings.

Nutrition information per serving: 287 calories, 11 g protein, 44 g carbohydrate, 8 g fat, 211 mg cholesterol, 392 mg sodium, 294 mg potassium.

*Note: To reduce calories, fat, and cholesterol, substitute 4 *egg whites* for the eggs; use *skim milk*. (239 calories, 3 g fat, 2 mg cholesterol per serving)

Strawberry-Rhubarb Sauce: In a medium saucepan stir together ⅔ cup *sugar* and 2 tablespoons *cornstarch*. Stir in ½ cup *water*. Add 1 cup fresh or frozen sliced *rhubarb* and 1 cup fresh or frozen sliced *strawberries*. Cook and stir till thickened and bubbly. Cook and stir for 2 minutes more. Remove from heat; stir in ½ cup fresh or frozen *raspberries or blueberries*. Makes 1½ cups sauce.

Nutrition information per tablespoon: 29 calories, 0 g protein, 7 g carbohydrate, 0 g fat, 0 mg cholesterol, 0 mg sodium, 36 mg potassium.

Here's a tasty recipe you can make ahead and keep in the freezer to pull out at a moment's notice. Bake the toast. Then, wrap the slices individually and freeze.
 To serve, unwrap and place the slices in a single layer on an ungreased baking sheet. Heat, uncovered, in a 400° oven for 6 to 8 minutes or till hot. For just a slice or two, reheat in the toaster.
 If you like, skip cooking the sauce and serve the toast with pancake syrup.

Keep 'Em Hot

Piping hot—that's when pancakes and waffles are at their best. So, keep the first ones toasty while you finish cooking the remaining batches.
 Place pancakes on a baking sheet or ovenproof plate in a 300° oven.
 Place waffles in a single layer on a wire rack. Set rack atop a baking sheet in a 300° oven.

Ham- and Swiss- Stuffed Toast

Total Time: 30 minutes

1 **16-ounce loaf French bread**	● Cut the French bread into ten to twelve 1-inch-thick slices. Cut a pocket in each bread slice, by making a cut in the center of each slice from the top almost to the bottom.

This knife-and-fork breakfast sandwich is a takeoff on the deli favorite, ham and Swiss on rye.

6 **slices Swiss *or* Havarti cheese (6 ounces total)** 2 **2½-ounce packages very thinly sliced smoked ham, chicken, *or* turkey**	● Fill *each* pocket with ½ *slice* of cheese and *some* of the ham, chicken, or turkey, dividing the meat evenly among the pockets.
4 **beaten eggs** 1 **cup milk** 1 **teaspoon vanilla** **Orange Syrup (optional)**	● In a bowl combine eggs, milk, and vanilla. Dip one stuffed bread slice in egg mixture, coating both sides and being careful not to squeeze out the filling. Place on a greased baking sheet. Repeat with remaining slices and egg mixture. Bake in a 450° oven for 8 minutes. Turn slices over and bake for 7 minutes more. If desired, serve warm Orange Syrup over slices. Makes 5 or 6 servings.

Nutrition information per serving: 530 calories, 29 g protein, 55 g carbohydrate, 20 g fat, 274 mg cholesterol, 1,069 mg sodium, 341 mg potassium.

Orange Syrup: In a small saucepan stir together ½ cup cold *water* and 4 teaspoons *cornstarch*. Stir in ½ teaspoon finely shredded *orange peel,* 1 cup *orange juice,* and 2 tablespoons *honey*. Cook and stir over medium heat till thickened and bubbly. Cook and stir for 2 minutes more. Makes about 1½ cups.

Nutrition information per tablespoon: 12 calories, 0 g protein, 3 g carbohydrate, 0 g fat, 0 mg cholesterol, 0 mg sodium, 21 mg potassium.

Micro- Warming Syrup

Warm syrup tastes great and helps keep pancakes and waffles hot. The quickest way to warm it is to use your microwave oven. Heat the syrup in a microwave-safe container, uncovered, on 100% power (high) till warm. Allow 30 to 60 seconds for ½ cup syrup and 1 to 1½ minutes for 1 cup syrup.

People-Pleasing Rolls

6¼ to 6¾ cups all-purpose flour	● In a large mixer bowl combine *3 cups* of the flour and the yeast.
2 packages active dry yeast	

1½ cups milk
½ cup margarine *or* butter
½ cup sugar
1 teaspoon salt
3 eggs

● In a saucepan heat milk, margarine, sugar, and salt just till warm (120° to 130°) and margarine is almost melted, stirring constantly. Add to flour mixture. Add eggs. Beat with an electric mixer on low speed for 30 seconds, scraping sides of bowl constantly. Beat on high speed for 3 minutes. Using a spoon, stir in as much of the remaining flour as you can.

Turn dough out onto a lightly floured surface. Knead in enough of the remaining flour to make a moderately stiff dough that is smooth and elastic (6 to 8 minutes total). Shape into a ball. Place in a greased bowl, turning once. Cover; let rise in a warm place till double (about 1 hour).

¾ cup sugar
½ cup margarine *or* butter, softened
4 teaspoons ground cinnamon *or* finely shredded orange peel
2 teaspoons all-purpose flour
¾ cup chopped nuts, miniature semisweet chocolate pieces, *or* raisins (optional)
Powdered Sugar Glaze (see recipe at far right)

● For filling, in a small bowl combine sugar, margarine or butter, cinnamon or orange peel, and flour; set aside.

Punch dough down; divide in half. Cover and let rest 10 minutes. On a lightly floured surface roll *each half* of the dough into a 12-inch square.

Spread *half* of the filling over *each* dough square. If desired, sprinkle with *half* of the nuts, chocolate, or raisins. Roll each square up jelly-roll style; pinch edges to seal. Slice each roll into 8 pieces. Place 8 pieces in a greased 13x9x2-inch baking pan. Repeat with remaining pieces using another 13x9x2-inch pan or a 12-inch pizza pan.

Cover loosely with clear plastic wrap, leaving room for rolls to rise. Refrigerate 2 to 24 hours. Uncover and let stand at room temperature for 30 minutes. (Or, don't chill dough. Instead, cover loosely; let rise in a warm place till nearly double, about 45 minutes). Break any surface bubbles with a greased toothpick.

Bake in a 375° oven for 20 to 25 minutes. Remove from pans. Cool slightly on a wire rack. Spread with Powdered Sugar Glaze. Makes 16 rolls.

Nutrition information per iced roll: 423 calories, 8 g protein, 68 g carbohydrate, 14 g fat, 53 mg cholesterol, 295 mg sodium, 125 mg potassium.

Imagine the wonderful aroma of freshly baked rolls. You can savor this aroma as well as delight in eating the rolls at your next brunch. How? It's a simple feat—let the dough rise overnight in the refrigerator. The next morning, give the rolls a little warm-up time at room temperature, then bake them till golden.

POWDERED SUGAR GLAZE: In a mixing bowl combine 2 cups sifted *powdered sugar* and ½ teaspoon *vanilla*. Add enough *milk* (2 to 3 tablespoons) to make of drizzling consistency.

Peach-Streusel Coffee Cake

1¼ cups all-purpose flour
⅔ cup sugar
½ teaspoon baking powder
½ teaspoon baking soda
¼ teaspoon ground nutmeg
¼ teaspoon ground ginger

● In a mixer bowl stir together flour, sugar, baking powder, baking soda, nutmeg, ginger, and ⅛ teaspoon *salt*.

½ cup buttermilk *or* sour milk
2 eggs
¼ cup shortening
½ teaspoon vanilla
2 cups sliced thawed frozen *or* canned peaches

● Add buttermilk or sour milk, eggs, shortening, and vanilla to dry ingredients in bowl. Beat with an electric mixer on low speed till combined, then on high speed for 2 minutes. Pour batter into a greased 9x9x2-inch baking pan.
 Drain peaches; slice any thick pieces. Arrange peach slices over batter.

¼ cup all-purpose flour
¼ cup quick-cooking rolled oats
¼ cup packed brown sugar
2 tablespoons margarine *or* butter

● For topping, in a small bowl combine flour, oats, and sugar. Cut in margarine till mixture resembles coarse crumbs. Sprinkle over peaches. Bake in a 350° oven for 35 to 40 minutes or till a toothpick inserted near the center comes out clean. Serve warm. Serves 9.

Nutrition information per serving: 275 calories, 5 g protein, 43 g carbohydrate, 10 g fat, 61 mg cholesterol, 170 mg sodium, 161 mg potassium.

Apricots make a great coffee cake, too! Just substitute a 16-ounce can of unpeeled apricot halves for the peaches. Drain and slice the apricots. Then, arrange them on the coffee cake batter.

Apple Coffee Ring

1½ cups all-purpose flour
¾ cup packed brown sugar
¾ teaspoon baking powder
¾ teaspoon baking soda
½ teaspoon ground cinnamon
¼ teaspoon ground nutmeg

● Grease and flour a 6-cup fluted tube pan or a 6½-cup ring mold. In a large mixing bowl stir together flour, sugar, baking powder, baking soda, cinnamon, nutmeg, and ¼ teaspoon *salt*.

1 beaten egg
1 8-ounce carton dairy sour cream
⅓ cup cooking oil
½ teaspoon vanilla
¾ cup finely chopped, peeled apple
⅓ cup raisins
¼ cup chopped pecans
 Sifted powdered sugar

● Stir together egg, sour cream, oil, and vanilla till well mixed. Add to dry ingredients; stir just till moistened. Stir in apple, raisins, and pecans. Pour batter into the prepared pan. Bake in a 350° oven for 35 to 40 minutes or till done.
 Cool in pan 5 minutes, then carefully unmold onto a rack to cool. Serve warm or cool. Sprinkle lightly with sifted powdered sugar. Makes 12 servings.

Nutrition information per serving: 245 calories, 3 g protein, 31 g carbohydrate, 12 g fat, 31 mg cholesterol, 154 mg sodium, 144 mg potassium.

If you like, mix and bake this coffee ring the day before. Cool it completely. Then, wrap and chill it.
 At brunch time, reheat the ring while you prepare the rest of the meal. Wrap it in foil and heat it in a 350° oven for 25 to 30 minutes.

Iced Apricot Coffee Cake

2 3-ounce packages cream cheese, softened **¼ cup sugar** **1 tablespoon lemon juice**	● For cheese filling, in a small mixing bowl beat together the cream cheese, sugar, and lemon juice; set aside.

So elegant—yet so easy. What's the secret? The base is frozen phyllo dough, the filling is a sweetened cream cheese mixture, and the topping is a tasty apricot or prune pastry filling.

6 sheets frozen phyllo dough (17x12-inch rectangles), thawed **¼ cup margarine *or* butter, melted**	● Unfold phyllo dough; remove *2* sheets. Cover remaining phyllo sheets with clear plastic wrap or a dampened towel. Layer the 2 sheets on a large (16x14-inch) baking sheet. Brush top sheet with some of the melted margarine. Layer two more sheets on first two; brush top sheet with margarine. Repeat with remaining sheets and margarine. Trim ends of dough to fit on baking sheet. On both long sides, make 4-inch cuts from edge toward center, spacing the cuts 1 inch apart.

½ cup apricot *or* prune cake and pastry filling
Powdered Sugar Icing (see recipe, far right)
	● Spoon the cheese filling lengthwise down the center of the phyllo stack. Spread into a 3-inch-wide strip.
	
	    Starting at one end, fold and twist the phyllo strips at an angle over the filling (*see photo, below*). Brush with any of the remaining margarine or butter.
	
	    Bake the coffee cake in a 375° oven for 25 to 30 minutes or till golden. Spoon the apricot or prune filling down the center of the coffee cake. Drizzle with Powdered Sugar Icing. Serve warm or cool. Makes 8 servings.

POWDERED SUGAR ICING: In a mixing bowl combine ½ cup sifted *powdered sugar* and ¼ teaspoon *vanilla*. Add enough *milk* (2 to 3 teaspoons) to make of drizzling consistency.

Nutrition information per serving: 224 calories, 2 g protein, 25 g carbohydrate, 30 g fat, 23 mg cholesterol, 176 mg sodium, 39 mg potassium.

Fold and twist each strip over the filling. Alternate from side to side, folding the strips at an angle over the filling as shown. This gives the coffee cake a ladderlike appearance.

Cranberry Ring

2¾ to 3¼ cups all-purpose
    flour
  1 package active dry yeast
  1 teaspoon ground
    cardamom
  ¼ teaspoon ground nutmeg
  ⅔ cup milk
  ⅓ cup sugar
  ¼ cup margarine *or* butter
  ¾ teaspoon salt
  1 egg

● In a mixer bowl combine *1¼ cups* of the flour, yeast, cardamom, and nutmeg.

In a saucepan heat milk, sugar, margarine or butter, and salt till warm (120° to 130°) and margarine is almost melted, stirring constantly. Add to flour mixture. Add egg. Beat with an electric mixer on low speed 30 seconds, scraping sides of bowl. Beat on high speed for 3 minutes. Using a spoon, stir in as much of the remaining flour as you can.

Turn out onto a floured surface. Knead in enough remaining flour to make a moderately soft dough that is smooth and elastic (6 to 8 minutes total). Shape into a ball. Place in a greased bowl; turn once. Cover; let rise in a warm place till double (1 to 1¼ hours).

1¼ cups cranberries
  ⅓ cup sugar
  1 tablespoon water
  1 teaspoon finely shredded
    orange peel
  ½ teaspoon ground
    cinnamon

● Meanwhile, in a saucepan combine cranberries, sugar, water, orange peel, and cinnamon. Cook and stir over medium heat till berries pop. Cook and stir 3 minutes more till very thick. Cover and cool the mixture.

Punch dough down; cover and let rest 10 minutes. On a lightly floured surface roll dough into an 18x9-inch rectangle. Spread with cranberry filling. Roll up jelly-roll style from long side. Seal edge.

On a greased baking sheet, shape in a ring; pinch to seal ends together. With kitchen shears, make cuts from outer edge almost to the center, making 12 pieces. Gently pull sections apart and twist dough on its side, overlapping slightly, as shown in photo. Cover and let rise till nearly double (about 30 minutes).

Bake in a 375° oven for 20 to 25 minutes, covering with foil the last 10 minutes to prevent overbrowning. Cool slightly on a wire rack before glazing.

Here are two ways you can make this special coffee cake ahead of time:

1. Bake the coffee cake and cool it completely. Skip the glaze, then wrap and freeze the coffee cake for up to 2 months. When ready to serve, bake the frozen coffee cake, loosely covered with foil, in a 350° oven for 25 to 30 minutes or till heated through. Then, cool slightly and add the glaze.

2. Prepare and shape the coffee cake the day before serving, *except* do not let it rise a second time. Then, cover and refrigerate the shaped dough overnight. The next morning, let the shaped dough stand at room temperature about 30 minutes. Bake, cool slightly, and add the glaze.

  1 cup sifted powdered sugar
  4 teaspoons milk
  ¼ teaspoon orange extract

● For glaze, combine powdered sugar, milk, and extract; drizzle over ring. Makes 12 servings.

Nutrition information per serving: 235 calories, 4 g protein, 44 g carbohydrate, 5 g fat, 24 mg cholesterol, 192 mg sodium, 80 mg potassium.

Giant Fruit Muffins

2 tablespoons all-purpose flour*
2 tablespoons brown sugar*
1 tablespoon margarine *or* butter*

● Lightly grease six 6-ounce custard cups or giant muffin cups. *Or,* line cups with large paper bake cups. Set aside.

For crumb topping, in a small bowl combine flour and brown sugar. Cut in margarine or butter till mixture resembles fine crumbs; set aside.

Make 'em with apples, or make 'em with blueberries. Either way, make 'em big!

1½ cups all-purpose flour
½ cup oat bran (see hint, page 37)
⅓ cup sugar
2½ teaspoons baking powder
¼ teaspoon salt

● In a mixing bowl combine flour, oat bran, sugar, baking powder, and salt. Make a well in the center of the dry ingredients.

---

2 beaten eggs*
¾ cup milk*
¼ cup cooking oil
1 teaspoon finely shredded orange peel
¾ cup chopped, peeled apple *or* fresh *or* frozen blueberries

● In another mixing bowl combine eggs, milk, oil, and orange peel. Add all at once to dry ingredients. Stir just till moistened (batter should be lumpy). Gently fold apple or berries into batter.

Divide batter among custard cups or giant muffin cups. Sprinkle with topping.

Bake in a 400° oven for 20 to 25 minutes or till golden and a toothpick comes out clean. Remove from cups. Serve warm. Makes 6 muffins.

Nutrition information per muffin: 367 calories, 8 g protein, 52 g carbohydrate, 14 g fat, 94 mg cholesterol, 272 mg sodium, 169 mg potassium.

***Note:* To reduce calories, fat, and cholesterol, substitute 2 slightly beaten *egg whites* for whole eggs and use *skim milk.* Omit crumb topping and combine 3 tablespoons *brown sugar* and ½ teaspoon ground *cinnamon;* sprinkle over muffins before baking. (324 calories, 10 g fat, 1 mg cholesterol per muffin)

Banana-Bran Muffins

1 beaten egg*	● Lightly grease 12 muffin cups or line with paper bake cups; set aside.
¾ cup buttermilk	
¾ cup mashed ripe banana	In a mixing bowl combine egg, buttermilk, banana, and oil. Stir in cereal; let stand 5 minutes.
¼ cup cooking oil	
1 cup whole bran cereal	

You'll notice that the muffin cups will be more than two-thirds full. The reason? These muffins don't rise as much as some others.

1½ cups all-purpose flour	● Meanwhile, in a large mixing bowl stir together flour, brown sugar, baking powder, baking soda, cinnamon, nutmeg, and ¼ teaspoon *salt*. Make a well in the center of the dry ingredients.
½ cup packed brown sugar	
1 teaspoon baking powder	
1 teaspoon baking soda	
½ teaspoon ground cinnamon	
¼ teaspoon ground nutmeg	

● Add banana-cereal mixture all at once to dry ingredients. Stir just till moistened (batter should be lumpy). Divide batter evenly among muffin cups.

Bake in a 400° oven for 18 to 20 minutes or till a toothpick comes out clean. (Or, cover and chill batter up to 24 hours in the refrigerator. Bake as directed.) Makes 12 muffins.

Nutrition information per muffin: 170 calories, 3 g protein, 28 g carbohydrate, 6 g fat, 23 mg cholesterol, 195 mg sodium, 189 mg potassium.

*__*Note:__ To reduce calories, fat, and cholesterol, substitute 2 slightly beaten *egg whites* for whole egg. (166 calories, 5 g fat, 1 mg cholesterol per muffin)

One Step Ahead

For those mornings when time is short, plan ahead by making extra muffins or pancakes. Wrap them and stash them in the freezer. Then, as the need arises, warm them in the microwave oven.

To thaw and reheat *frozen* muffins: Place on a microwave-safe plate. Heat, uncovered, on 100% power (high) till warm. Allow 30 to 45 seconds for 1 or 2 muffins and 70 to 75 seconds for 4 muffins.

To thaw and reheat *frozen* pancakes: Stack on a microwave-safe plate. Heat, uncovered, on 100% power (high) till warm. Allow 40 to 45 seconds for 1 or 2 pancakes and 60 to 90 seconds for 3 or 4 cakes.

Bacon Popovers

3 slices bacon *or*
   3 tablespoons grated
   Parmesan cheese
1 tablespoon shortening

● If using bacon, cook bacon till crisp; drain, reserving 1 tablespoon drippings, if desired. Finely crumble bacon. Set aside. Using ½ teaspoon shortening for *each* cup, grease the bottom and sides of six cups of a popover pan. (Or, use six 6-ounce custard cups. Place greased custard cups in a 15x10x1-inch baking pan.) Set aside.

Want to know what makes popovers pop?
   It's the steam that forms when they bake at a high temperature. The resulting perfect popover should be golden brown and crispy on the outside and hollow with a tender, moist lining inside.

2 beaten eggs
1 cup milk
1 tablespoon cooking oil *or*
   bacon drippings
1 cup all-purpose flour

● In a mixing bowl combine eggs, milk, and oil or bacon drippings. Add flour and bacon or Parmesan cheese. Beat with a rotary beater or wire whisk till mixture is smooth. Fill the prepared cups half full. Bake in a 400° oven about 40 minutes or till very firm.
   Immediately, remove popovers from the oven and prick each with a fork to let steam escape. (If crisper popovers are desired, after baking, prick the popovers, turn the oven off, and leave popovers in the oven for 5 to 10 minutes more or till of desired crispness.) Serve hot. Makes 6.

Nutrition information per popover: 183 calories, 7 g protein, 18 g carbohydrate, 9 g fat, 98 mg cholesterol, 104 mg sodium, 123 mg potassium.

Herb Popovers: Prepare as above, *except* omit bacon or cheese. Stir 1 tablespoon finely chopped fresh *dillweed or basil* or ¾ teaspoon dried *dillweed or basil,* crushed, into batter before pouring into prepared cups.

Nutrition information per popover: 161 calories, 6 g protein, 18 g carbohydrate, 7 g fat, 95 mg cholesterol, 44 mg sodium, 108 mg potassium.

Bagel Toppings

For a quick breakfast treat, create one of these bagel concoctions:
● Scramble some *eggs* and add sliced *cooked sausage.* Spoon the mixture over split, toasted *bagels.*
● Mix *soft-style cream cheese* with *dried fruit bits, nuts,* and a dash *ground cinnamon.* Spread on split *bagels.*
● Spread *peanut butter* on split *bagels.* Top with *apple* slices and *cinnamon-sugar.*

Wheat and Oat Biscuits

Total Time: 25 minutes

¾ cup all-purpose flour
¾ cup whole wheat flour
½ cup oat bran
1 tablespoon baking powder
1 tablespoon sugar
¼ teaspoon salt
½ cup margarine *or* butter

● In a mixing bowl stir together all-purpose flour, whole wheat flour, oat bran, baking powder, sugar, and salt. Cut in margarine or butter till mixture resembles coarse crumbs.

1 beaten egg
½ cup milk

● Make a well in the center of dry ingredients. Combine egg and milk. Add all at once to dry ingredients; mix just till dough clings together. On a well-floured surface gently knead dough for 10 to 12 strokes. Roll or pat dough to ½-inch thickness. Cut with a 2½-inch biscuit cutter, dipping cutter into flour between cuts; place on ungreased baking sheet.

Honey-Lemon Butter (see recipe, far right) (optional)

● Bake in a 425° oven for 12 to 15 minutes. Serve with Honey-Lemon Butter, if desired. Makes 10.

Nutrition information per biscuit: 177 calories, 4 g protein, 17 g carbohydrate, 10 g fat, 28 mg cholesterol, 265 mg sodium, 88 mg potassium.

These hearty biscuits taste especially delicious with HONEY-LEMON BUTTER: In a small mixer bowl beat together ½ cup *margarine or butter* and ½ teaspoon finely shredded *lemon peel* till light and fluffy. Beat in ¼ cup *honey*. Makes ¾ cup.

Parmesan-Chive Spirals

Total Time: 25 minutes

Pictured on pages 54 and 55.

1 11-ounce package (8) refrigerated breadsticks

● Separate breadsticks into individual pieces. For each piece, bring the opposite ends of the stick together. Twist into a spiral.

3 tablespoons grated Parmesan cheese
2 teaspoons snipped chives

● Carefully dip one side of each spiral into a mixture of cheese and chives. Place spirals, cheese side up, on a greased baking sheet. Sprinkle with any remaining cheese mixture. Bake in a 350° oven about 15 minutes or till golden. Serve warm. Makes 4 servings.

Nutrition information per serving: 222 calories, 9 g protein, 33 g carbohydrate, 6 g fat, 4 mg cholesterol, 553 mg sodium, 55 mg potassium.

Give these refrigerated breadsticks two different twists. First, spiral them for a twisted look. Then, top them with Parmesan cheese and chives for a flavor twist.

Spicy Bran Wedges

1 cup whole bran cereal
½ cup buttermilk *or* sour milk
1 beaten egg
1 egg white
½ cup margarine *or* butter, melted and cooled

● In a medium mixing bowl combine cereal and buttermilk or sour milk; let stand for 3 minutes or till milk is absorbed. Stir in egg, egg white, and melted margarine or butter. Set aside.

2 cups all-purpose flour
⅓ cup sugar
1 tablespoon baking powder
1 teaspoon apple pie spice *or* ground cinnamon

● In a large mixing bowl combine flour, sugar, baking powder, and spice. Make a well in the center of the dry ingredients. Add bran-egg mixture; mix just till dough clings together.

On a floured surface, gently knead dough for 10 to 15 strokes or till smooth and well blended. Divide dough in half. On a large ungreased baking sheet roll or pat *each* half of the dough into a 6½-inch circle.

1 egg yolk
1 tablespoon milk
1 tablespoon sugar
½ teaspoon apple pie spice *or* ground cinnamon

● Stir together egg yolk and milk. Brush over tops of circles. Combine sugar and spice; sprinkle over circles. Cut each circle into 6 or 12 wedges and leave wedges in the circle.

Bake in a 425° oven for 12 to 14 minutes or till golden brown. Gently cut through to separate. Serve warm. Makes 12 or 24 wedges.

Nutrition information per large wedge: 201 calories, 4 g protein, 27 g carbohydrate, 9 g fat, 46 mg cholesterol, 240 mg sodium, 112 mg potassium.

Since this recipe makes a lot, put the leftovers in the freezer for an easy breakfast another day. To serve, place frozen wedges on a baking sheet. Loosely cover with foil and bake in a 350° oven for 15 to 20 minutes or till warm.

Menu

Autumn Brunch

Stage a brunch that allows plenty of time for afternoon activities, such as the theater or a football game. Just follow the preparation timetable. Since the menu is for four, you'll find it's manageable as a sit-down meal.

Egg- and Rice-Stuffed Peppers
(see recipe, page 57)

Spinach and Pea Pod Toss
(see recipe, page 56)

MENU

Pineapple-orange juice

Egg- and Rice-Stuffed Peppers

Spinach and Pea Pod Toss

Parmesan-Chive Spirals

Coffee *or* Tea

Parmesan-Chive Spirals
(see recipe, page 52)

Autumn Brunch

Menu

Pineapple-orange juice
Egg- and Rice-Stuffed
   Peppers
Spinach and Pea Pod Toss
Parmesan-Chive Spirals
   (see recipe, page 52)
Coffee *or* Tea

MENU COUNTDOWN

Several Hours Ahead:
Hard-cook the eggs for
Egg- and Rice-Stuffed
Peppers; chill. Chill
pineapple-orange juice.
1¼ Hours Ahead:
Start to prepare
peppers.
50 Minutes Ahead:
Prepare the pea pods
and spinach for the
Spinach and Pea Pod
Toss; toss vegetables with
pimiento. Cover and chill
till serving time.
45 Minutes Ahead:
Preheat the oven.

35 Minutes Ahead:
Place peppers in oven to
heat.
30 Minutes Ahead:
Prepare and bake Parmesan-
Chive Spirals.
15 Minutes Ahead:
Cook sauce for peppers.
Prepare coffee or tea.
Just Before Serving:
Combine salad dressing
ingredients. Toss vegetables
with almonds and dressing.
Pour the chilled juice. Spoon
sauce over peppers.

Total Time: 15 minutes

Spinach and Pea Pod Toss

Pictured on pages 54 and 55.

1	**6-ounce package frozen pea pods**
3	**cups torn fresh spinach**
2	**tablespoons sliced pimiento**

● Rinse pea pods under water till
thawed. Drain. Cut pea pods in half
crosswise. In a salad bowl place spinach,
pea pods, and pimiento.

**When using this salad for
the Autumn Brunch, plan
to serve it right on the
plate with the stuffed
peppers to cut down on
dishwashing.**

3	**tablespoons salad oil**
2	**tablespoons vinegar**
2	**teaspoons soy sauce**
1	**teaspoon honey**
1	**tablespoon sliced almonds**

● For the dressing, in a jar combine
salad oil, vinegar, soy sauce, and honey.
Cover and shake well. Add almonds to
salad. Pour dressing over spinach
mixture; toss and serve immediately.
Makes 4 servings.

Nutrition information per serving: 134 calories,
3 g protein, 8 g carbohydrate, 11 g fat, 0 mg
cholesterol, 209 mg sodium, 327 mg potassium.

Egg- and Rice-Stuffed Peppers

Pictured on pages 54 and 55.

2 large red *or* green sweet peppers	● Cut peppers in half lengthwise. Remove stems, seeds, and membranes. In a large saucepan cook peppers, covered, in a large amount of boiling water for 3 minutes. Invert peppers on paper towels to drain.
4 hard-cooked eggs **3 tablespoons mayonnaise *or* salad dressing** **1 tablespoon snipped parsley** **¼ teaspoon dry mustard**	● Remove shells from eggs; halve eggs lengthwise. Remove and mash yolks with a fork or a potato masher; set whites aside. Stir mayonnaise or salad dressing, parsley, and dry mustard into egg yolks.
1 10-ounce package frozen long grain and wild rice	● Arrange peppers, cut side up, in an 8x8x2-inch baking dish. Run frozen rice in bag under running water to thaw. Spoon *one-fourth* of the rice into *each* pepper cup. Spoon egg yolk mixture on top of rice in center of peppers. Cut each egg white half into 2 wedges; place *4* wedges atop *each* stuffed pepper cup. Cover baking dish loosely with foil. Bake in a 350° oven for 35 to 40 minutes or till heated through.
1 tablespoon margarine *or* butter **1 tablespoon all-purpose flour** **¾ cup milk** **¾ cup shredded American cheese (3 ounces)**	● Meanwhile, in a small saucepan melt margarine or butter. Stir in flour till combined. Add milk all at once. Cook and stir over medium heat till mixture is thickened and bubbly. Cook and stir for 1 minute more. Stir cheese into the sauce till melted.
	● To serve, spoon some of the sauce atop stuffed peppers; pass remaining sauce. Makes 4 servings.

Nutrition information per serving: 388 calories, 15 g protein, 24 g carbohydrate, 26 g fat, 303 mg cholesterol, 836 mg sodium, 368 mg potassium.

Although the menu countdown tells you when to prepare this main dish on the day of the brunch, you can save time by stuffing the peppers the day before. Cover and chill them overnight in the refrigerator. Then in the morning bake them, loosely covered, in a 350° oven about 40 minutes or till hot.

MICROWAVE TIMING: Use a microwave-safe 8x8x2-inch baking dish. Cover stuffed peppers loosely with waxed paper. Micro-cook on 100% power (high) for 5 to 7 minutes or till heated through, giving dish a half-turn after 3 minutes. Prepare sauce on range top as directed.

Mushroom-Stuffed Tomatoes

Total Time: 25 minutes

2 **large tomatoes** ⅛ **teaspoon salt**	● Cut tomatoes in half, crosswise. Scoop out centers, leaving shell about ¼ inch thick. Sprinkle insides of tomatoes with salt. Invert tomatoes on paper towels; set aside.
2 **cups sliced fresh mushrooms** 2 **tablespoons sliced green onion** 2 **tablespoons oil and vinegar salad dressing with herbs and spices**	● In a medium skillet cook mushrooms and green onion in salad dressing until vegetables are tender.
1 **cup soft bread crumbs** ¼ **cup grated Parmesan cheese** 3 **tablespoons margarine *or* butter, melted**	● In a mixing bowl combine crumbs, cheese, and melted margarine or butter. Reserve *½ cup* of the crumb mixture. Stir the remaining crumbs into mushroom mixture. Fill tomatoes with mushroom mixture. Top with reserved crumbs. Broil 4 to 5 inches from the heat for 3 to 5 minutes or until topping is golden. Serves 4.

Nutrition information per serving: 191 calories, 5 g protein, 11 g carbohydrate, 14 g fat, 5 mg cholesterol, 450 mg sodium, 288 mg potassium.

Add a splash of color to a brunch featuring scrambled eggs or omelets with these luscious, stuffed tomatoes. For best serving size, select tomatoes measuring 3 to 3½ inches in diameter. You can prepare the tomato shells up to 4 hours ahead of time. Just invert the hollowed out halves on paper towels and then cover and refrigerate.

Rainbow Fruit Surprise

6 medium peaches *or* nectarines (1½ pounds), peeled, pitted, and sliced, *or* 3 cups frozen unsweetened peach slices, thawed **1 tablespoon lemon juice**	● In a large mixing bowl toss *2 cups* of the peaches or nectarines with lemon juice; set aside.
⅓ cup water **1 tablespoon lemon juice**	● In a medium saucepan combine remaining sliced peaches or nectarines, water, and lemon juice. Bring to boiling; reduce heat. Cover and simmer about 5 minutes or till very tender. *Do not drain.* Cool the mixture slightly. Place slightly cooled mixture in a blender container or food processor bowl. Process till mixture is smooth. Return to saucepan.
3 tablespoons sugar **2 teaspoons cornstarch** **Dash ground cinnamon** **Dash ground cloves**	● In a small mixing bowl combine sugar, cornstarch, cinnamon, and cloves. Add to pureed peach mixture in the saucepan. Cook and stir till mixture is thickened and bubbly; cook and stir for 2 minutes more. Cool.
1 pound plums, pitted, quartered, and cut into bite-size pieces **1 cup seedless green grapes, halved** **1½ cups blueberries** **1 medium banana, sliced**	● Combine the reserved peaches or nectarines, plums, and grapes. Spoon peach sauce over all. Toss gently to coat. Cover and chill up to 4 hours. At serving time, add blueberries and banana; toss to mix. Serve immediately. Makes 8 servings.

Nutrition information per serving: 122 calories, 1 g protein, 31 g carbohydrate, 1 g fat, 0 mg cholesterol, 2 mg sodium, 344 mg potassium.

What's so surprising about this colorful five-fruit medley? Why, it's the spicy peach sauce that coats the fruit.

**   For a smaller brunch, cut the recipe in half and use one small banana.**

Fig-Peach Tarts

2 sheets frozen phyllo dough
   (17x12-inch rectangles),
   thawed
2 tablespoons margarine *or*
   butter, melted

● Brush *one* sheet of phyllo dough with some of the melted margarine or butter. Top with remaining phyllo dough sheet; repeat brushing. Cut phyllo in half crosswise and stack atop other rectangle, making a 12x8½-inch 4-sheet stack. Cut phyllo stack lengthwise in half; cut crosswise into 6 pieces, each about 4 inches square.
   Press one square stack into each of 6 greased muffin cups. Bake in a 350° oven for 12 to 15 minutes or till golden. Remove from muffin cups and cool completely on a wire rack.

Beat the brunch-day clock by baking the phyllo cups up to several weeks ahead. Carefully pack the delicate cups in a freezer container and freeze.
   When you're ready to use them, let the cups thaw at room temperature a few minutes.

½ of an 8-ounce package
   dried figs, quartered
   (¾ cup)
½ cup water
¼ cup light raisins
¼ cup orange juice
2 teaspoons sugar
1½ teaspoons lemon juice
3 medium peaches, peeled,
   pitted, and sliced
   (1½ cups), *or* 1½ cups
   frozen unsweetened
   peach slices, thawed

● For filling, in a saucepan combine figs, water, raisins, orange juice, sugar, and lemon juice. Bring to boiling; reduce heat. Simmer, uncovered, for 5 minutes. Stir in peaches. Cook, uncovered, about 2 minutes more or till peaches are tender, stirring occasionally.

1 tablespoon cold water
2 teaspoons cornstarch
¼ cup dairy sour cream
   Ground cinnamon
   (optional)

● Stir water into cornstarch. Stir into filling. Cook and stir till thickened and bubbly. Cook and stir for 2 minutes more. To serve, spoon warm filling into phyllo shells. Top with a dollop of sour cream. If desired, sprinkle lightly with cinnamon. Makes 6 servings.

Nutrition information per serving: 162 calories, 2 g protein, 27 g carbohydrate, 14 g fat, 4 mg cholesterol, 71 mg sodium, 304 mg potassium

Tropical Fruit Medley

1 **8-ounce can pineapple tidbits (juice pack)**	● In a bowl combine *undrained* pineapple, orange juice, crystallized ginger, and lemon juice.
⅓ **cup orange juice**	
1 **tablespoon chopped crystallized ginger**	
2 **teaspoons lemon juice**	

Tropical ingredients in this fruit combo conjure up images of palm trees swaying in the breeze. What a wonderful way to start the day!

1 **mango** *or* **papaya**	● Peel the mango or papaya and remove pit or seeds; cut fruit into cubes. Peel and diagonally slice banana. Peel and slice kiwi fruit. Add fruits to pineapple mixture in bowl. Toss gently to coat. Cover and chill about 1 hour. Divide fruit and sauce among 4 bowls. Sprinkle with coconut. Makes 4 servings.
1 **banana**	
1 **kiwi fruit**	
¼ **cup toasted coconut**	

Nutrition information per serving: 152 calories, 1 g protein, 35 g carbohydrate, 2 g fat, 0 mg cholesterol, 6 mg sodium, 489 mg potassium.

SUPER FAST

Total Time: 15 minutes

Honeyed Grapefruit

¼ **cup frozen orange juice concentrate, thawed**	● In a medium mixing bowl combine orange juice concentrate, water, honey, and poppy seed. Stir till ingredients are mixed thoroughly.
¼ **cup water**	
2 **tablespoons honey**	
½ **teaspoon poppy seed**	

Section a grapefruit by cutting into the center of the peeled fruit between one section and the membrane. Twist knife and continue outward, cutting section free from the other side of the membrane, as shown. Work over a bowl to catch juices and fruit sections.

2 **large grapefruit**	● Peel and section grapefruit into the bowl with orange juice mixture (see photo at right). Toss to coat fruit with juice mixture. Chill till serving time. Divide fruit mixture among 4 bowls. Makes 4 servings.

Nutrition information per serving: 79 calories, 1 g protein, 20 g carbohydrate, 0 g fat, 0 mg cholesterol, 1 mg sodium, 204 mg potassium.

Poached Apples with Crème Fraîche

Crème Fraîche (see recipe at far right) *or* one 8-ounce carton vanilla yogurt

● If using Crème Fraîche, prepare it at least 24 hours before serving.

6 medium cooking apples
¾ cup water
½ cup sugar
1 tablespoon lemon juice
¼ teaspoon ground nutmeg
¼ teaspoon ground ginger
2 tablespoons cream sherry (optional)

● Peel, core, and cut apples into wedges. Set apples aside.
  In a 10-inch skillet combine water, sugar, lemon juice, nutmeg, and ginger. Add sherry, if desired. Bring to boiling.
  Add apples. Return to boiling, then reduce heat. Cover and simmer for 5 to 8 minutes or till apples are tender. Cool slightly. Divide apples and syrup among 6 individual bowls. Spoon thickened crème fraîche or vanilla yogurt on top. Serve at once. If desired, garnish with a lemon peel twist. Serves 6.

Nutrition information per serving with Crème Fraîche: 286 calories, 1 g protein, 39 g carbohydrate, 15 g fat, 55 mg cholesterol, 20 mg sodium, 201 mg potassium.

CRÈME FRAÎCHE: In a small saucepan heat 1 cup *whipping cream* over low heat till warm (90° to 100°). Pour into a small bowl. Stir in 2 tablespoons *buttermilk*. Cover; let stand at room temperature for 24 to 30 hours or till mixture is thickened. *Do not stir.* (This mixture can be stored in a covered container in the refrigerator for up to one week.) Stir before serving. Makes 1 cup.

SUPER *FAST*

Total Time: 10 minutes

Banana-Berry Whip

2 small ripe bananas, cut up
⅔ cup orange juice

● In a blender container combine bananas and orange juice. Cover and blend till fruit is pureed.

1 pint (2 cups) raspberry sherbet
6 ice cubes

● Add sherbet. Cover and blend till smooth. With blender running, add ice cubes through opening in lid, blending till smooth and of desired consistency. Pour mixture into 4 stemmed glasses. If desired, garnish with a piece of fresh fruit. Serve immediately with short straws. Makes 4 (7-ounce) servings.

Nutrition information per serving: 210 calories, 2 g protein, 48 g carbohydrate, 2 g fat, 7 mg cholesterol, 45 mg sodium, 423 mg potassium.

Whirl your breakfast fruit together, then drink it from a glass. It's simple to make . . . delightful to sip.

Tossed Hearts of Palm Salad

  3 tablespoons salad oil
  3 tablespoons tarragon
     vinegar
  ½ teaspoon sugar
  ¼ teaspoon salt
  ¼ teaspoon dry mustard
  ⅛ teaspoon pepper
  2 tablespoons capers,
     drained (optional)
  1 14-ounce can hearts of
     palm, drained

● For the dressing, in a screw-top jar combine salad oil, vinegar, sugar, salt, mustard, and pepper. Add capers, if desired. Cover and shake well to mix.

Cut hearts of palm into ½-inch slices and place in a shallow bowl. Pour dressing over hearts of palm. Cover and chill in the refrigerator for 2 to 24 hours, stirring once or twice.

Not familiar with hearts of palm? They're the young buds of a palm tree, most commonly the cabbage palm. By themselves, they have a delicate flavor. But add them to this well-seasoned marinade and they'll pick up lots of other flavors, too.

  4 cups torn lettuce
  2 cups torn curly endive *or*
     fresh spinach
  1½ cups cherry tomatoes

● In a large salad bowl combine lettuce and endive or spinach. Halve cherry tomatoes; add to bowl. Pour hearts of palm and dressing mixture over the salad. Toss lightly to coat. Serves 6.

Nutrition information per serving: 131 calories, 3 g protein, 17 g carbohydrate, 7 g fat, 0 mg cholesterol, 109 mg sodium, 1,164 mg potassium.

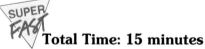

Total Time: 15 minutes

Wilted Savoy Salad

  1 6-ounce jar marinated
     artichoke hearts
  ½ cup fully cooked ham cut
     into julienne strips
  1 small green pepper, cut
     into thin strips

● Drain artichokes, reserving marinade. Cut up any large artichoke pieces.

In a 10-inch skillet heat reserved marinade. Add ham and pepper strips. Cook and stir for 2 minutes or till peppers are crisp-tender. Add artichokes; toss to coat.

This wilted salad is the perfect side dish for eggs.

  4 cups torn Savoy cabbage *or*
     Chinese cabbage
  ¼ teaspoon celery seed
  1 medium tomato, cut into
     wedges
     Freshly ground pepper

● Stir in the cabbage and celery seed. Cook over low heat about 2 minutes, tossing just till cabbage wilts. Garnish with tomato wedges. Sprinkle with pepper. Makes 4 servings.

Nutrition information per serving: 117 calories, 6 g protein, 11 g carbohydrate, 6 g fat, 9 mg cholesterol, 404 mg sodium, 406 mg potassium.

Total Time: 20 minutes

Fruited Greens

4 cups torn mixed greens
1 medium pear, cored and
   sliced into thin wedges
1 medium carrot, thinly
   biased sliced
¼ cup chopped pitted dates
¼ cup pecan halves

● Place greens on a serving platter. Arrange pear wedges and carrot slices on greens. Sprinkle with dates and pecans.

Pears, dates, and salad greens may sound like an unusual combination. But, we've turned them into a great-tasting brunch salad. The sweetened dressing adds the perfect finishing touch.

⅓ cup orange yogurt
2 tablespoons mayonnaise
   or salad dressing*
1 tablespoon orange
   marmalade

● For dressing, in a small mixing bowl combine yogurt, mayonnaise or salad dressing, and marmalade. To serve, drizzle dressing over salad. Serves 4.

Nutrition information per serving: 174 calories, 3 g protein, 25 g carbohydrate, 8 g fat, 3 mg cholesterol, 42 mg sodium, 391 mg potassium.

*__Note:__ To reduce calories, fat, and cholesterol, substitute reduced-calorie mayonnaise or salad dressing for the regular products. (160 calories, 7 g fat, 2 mg cholesterol per serving)

Total Time: 20 minutes

Orange and Spinach Toss

4 cups torn fresh spinach *or*
   torn mixed greens
1 11-ounce can mandarin
   orange sections,
   drained
3 kumquats, thinly sliced
   (optional)

● In a salad bowl toss together spinach or mixed greens, drained oranges, and kumquats, if desired.

If you add kumquats to the salad, remember you can eat them skin and all.

2 tablespoons orange juice
1 teaspoon lemon juice
¼ of an 8-ounce container
   (¼ cup) soft-style
   cream cheese with
   strawberries
¼ cup toasted coconut

● For dressing, gradually stir orange juice and lemon juice into cream cheese, beating, if necessary, till smooth.
   To serve, toss dressing with spinach and fruit mixture. Sprinkle with coconut. Makes 4 servings.

Nutrition information per serving: 110 calories, 3 g protein, 11 g carbohydrate, 7 g fat, 0 mg cholesterol, 81 mg sodium, 439 mg potassium.

Homemade Breakfast Cereals

For breakfasts starring cereal, stir together your own combinations to keep on hand.

GRAIN AND FRUIT CEREAL: In an airtight storage container stir together 1 cup *cornmeal,* ⅔ cup *bulgur,* one 6-ounce package mixed *dried fruit bits,* ½ cup *slivered almonds,* toasted, and ½ teaspoon *ground cinnamon.* Cover and store in the refrigerator up to 1 month. Makes 2⅔ cups.

   To cook 1 serving: In a small saucepan bring 1 cup *water* and a dash *salt* to boiling. Slowly stir in ⅓ cup cereal mixture. Simmer, uncovered, about 10 minutes or to desired consistency. Serve with *sugar* and *milk.* (To make 2 servings, prepare cereal as directed, *except* use *2 cups* water, ⅛ *teaspoon* salt, and ⅔ *cup* cereal mixture. Double proportions to make 4 servings.)

Nutrition information per serving (without sugar and milk): 192 calories, 5 g protein, 36 g carbohydrate, 4 g fat, 0 mg cholesterol, 138 mg sodium, 306 mg potassium.

BRAN AND NUT CEREAL: In an airtight storage container stir together 1 cup *bran flakes,* 1 cup *corn bran cereal,* ½ cup *wheat germ or toasted wheat bran,* ⅔ cup chopped *walnuts,* ⅓ cup snipped pitted *whole dates,* ⅓ cup snipped *dried apple,* ¼ cup *unsalted sunflower nuts,* and ¼ cup *dried banana chips,* crushed. Cover and store in the refrigerator for up to 1 month. Serve with *milk.* Makes about 5 cups.

Nutrition information per ½ cup (without milk): 141 calories, 4 g protein, 20 g carbohydrate, 7 g fat, 0 mg cholesterol, 98 mg sodium, 272 mg potassium.

Lemon-Sauced Vegetables

Total Time: 15 minutes

1 pound fresh *or* frozen snap peas *or* frozen cut green beans

● If using fresh peas, snip ends and remove strings. In a saucepan cook peas, covered, in a small amount of boiling water for 5 to 6 minutes or till tender. (If using frozen peas or beans, cook according to package directions.) Drain. Cover and keep warm.

1 tablespoon margarine *or* butter
2 teaspoons cornstarch
⅛ teaspoon salt
   Dash white pepper
⅔ cup milk
1½ teaspoons finely shredded lemon peel

● Meanwhile, in a small saucepan melt margarine or butter. Stir in cornstarch, salt, and pepper. Add the milk all at once. Cook and stir till thickened and bubbly. Cook and stir for 2 minutes more. Stir in lemon peel. Serve over drained vegetables. Makes 6 servings.

Nutrition information per serving: 57 calories, 2 g protein, 8 g carbohydrate, 3 g fat, 2 mg cholesterol, 85 mg sodium, 201 mg potassium.

For a tasty brunch, serve these creamy vegetables with Canadian-style bacon slices, poached eggs, and toasted English muffins.

Broiled Parmesan Potatoes

Total Time: 25 minutes

2 tablespoons margarine *or* butter, melted
1 teaspoon dried basil, crushed
½ teaspoon paprika
¼ teaspoon garlic powder
⅛ teaspoon pepper

● In a small mixing bowl stir together margarine or butter, basil, paprika, garlic powder, and pepper.

2 medium potatoes, bias sliced about ¼ inch thick
¼ cup grated Parmesan *or* Romano cheese

● Place potato slices in a single layer on the unheated rack of a broiler pan. Brush margarine mixture over both sides of potato slices. Broil about 5 inches from the heat for 8 to 9 minutes or till potatoes begin to brown.
   Using a wide spatula, turn potatoes. Sprinkle with cheese. Broil for 4 to 6 minutes more or till potatoes are tender. Makes 4 servings.

Nutrition information per serving: 164 calories, 5 g protein, 20 g carbohydrate, 8 g fat, 5 mg cholesterol, 367 mg sodium, 344 mg potassium.

Thinly slice the unpeeled potatoes so they'll cook evenly without burning.

Spiced Chocolate Eggnog

Total Time: 15 minutes

---

4 cups dairy eggnog or
　　canned eggnog
2 cups milk
⅓ cup chocolate-flavored
　　syrup
¼ teaspoon ground nutmeg
⅛ teaspoon ground allspice

● In a large saucepan combine eggnog, milk, chocolate-flavored syrup, nutmeg, and allspice. Heat through.

The whipped cream, crème de menthe, and chocolate curls really dress up this chocolate-flavored eggnog.

Whipping cream, whipped,
　　or whipped dessert
　　topping (optional)
Green crème de menthe *or*
　　green crème de menthe
　　syrup (optional)
Chocolate curls (optional)

● Pour into mugs. If desired, top each serving with whipped cream topping, drizzle with a little crème de menthe or syrup, and add chocolate curls. Makes 8 (6-ounce) servings.

Nutrition information per serving: 232 calories, 7 g protein, 28 g carbohydrate, 11 g fat, 79 mg cholesterol, 106 mg sodium, 340 mg potassium.

Apple-Cot Punch

Total Time: 5 minutes

---

1 750-milliliter bottle
　　sparkling apple cider,
　　chilled
1 12-ounce can apricot
　　nectar, chilled
　　Ice cubes

● In a pitcher combine the sparkling cider and nectar. Stir gently. Serve over ice. If desired, garnish with a fruit kabob, threading grapes and apricot wedges on a skewer. Makes 6 (6-ounce) servings.

Nutrition information per serving: 93 calories, 0 g protein, 23 g carbohydrate, 0 g fat, 0 mg cholesterol, 6 mg sodium, 217 mg potassium.

Sparkling cider adds a bubbly apple flavor to apricot nectar.

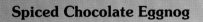

Spiced Chocolate Eggnog

Fruited Iced Tea
(see recipe, page 72)

Apple-Cot Punch

Fruited Iced Tea

Pictured on page 71.

3 tablespoons instant tea powder
4 cups cold water

● In a pitcher dissolve tea in water.

Start with all cold ingredients and you can serve this fruity, tart tea right away.

1½ cups unsweetened pineapple juice, chilled
1 6-ounce can frozen limeade concentrate
Ice cubes
Fresh mint sprigs (optional)

● Stir in pineapple juice and limeade concentrate till combined. To serve, pour over ice cubes in tall glasses. Garnish with fresh mint sprigs, if desired. Makes 6 (8-ounce) servings.

Nutrition information per serving: 106 calories, 0 g protein, 28 g carbohydrate, 0 g fat, 0 mg cholesterol, 1 mg sodium, 182 mg potassium.

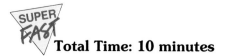

Total Time: 10 minutes

Citrus Eye-Opener

Pictured on the cover.

1 12-ounce can (1½ cups) frozen orange juice concentrate
1 6-ounce can (¾ cup) frozen lemonade concentrate
1½ cups cold water

● In a large container combine orange juice concentrate, lemonade concentrate, and water.

Two fruit concentrates—orange juice and lemonade—give punch to this brunch drink.

1 1-liter bottle carbonated water, chilled
Ice cubes
Orange slices, halved (optional)

● Just before serving, slowly add carbonated water. Stir gently to mix. Serve over ice cubes. Garnish with orange slice halves, if desired. Makes 8 (7- to 8-ounce) servings.

Nutrition information per serving: 137 calories, 1 g protein, 34 g carbohydrate, 0 g fat, 0 mg cholesterol, 2 mg sodium, 378 mg potassium.

Total Time: 25 minutes

Spiced Maple Tea

2 inches stick cinnamon
2 2x1-inch strips orange peel with white removed
1 teaspoon whole cloves
3 cups water

● For spice bag, place cinnamon, peel, and cloves on a piece of clean 100% cotton cheesecloth for cooking; tie into a bag. In a medium saucepan combine water and the spice bag. Bring to boiling; reduce heat. Simmer, covered, for 10 minutes. Remove spice bag and discard.

2 tea bags
¼ cup maple-flavored syrup

● Pour spiced water mixture over tea bags in a teapot. Cover pot and let steep 5 minutes. Remove tea bags. Stir in the syrup and serve at once. If desired, chill the mixture and serve over ice. Makes 4 (6-ounce) servings.

Nutrition information per serving: 52 calories, 0 g protein, 14 g carbohydrate, 0 g fat, 0 mg cholesterol, 2 mg sodium, 73 mg potassium.

No cheesecloth? Add the spices and orange peel right to the tea mixture. Then, after simmering, strain the tea through a sieve to remove spices and peel.

Total Time: 5 minutes

Tangerine Bubbly

2 cups cold water
1 6-ounce can frozen tangerine juice concentrate *or* orange juice concentrate
2 tablespoons sugar

● In a pitcher combine water, frozen juice concentrate, and sugar; stir till thoroughly mixed.

1 750-milliliter bottle champagne, chilled

● Slowly pour in champagne. Stir gently to mix. Serve in glasses or punch cups. If desired, serve over ice. Makes 12 (4-ounce) servings.

Nutrition information per serving: 89 calories, 0 g protein, 11 g carbohydrate, 0 g fat, 0 mg cholesterol, 4 mg sodium, 177 mg potassium.

For a midday brunch, serve this fruited champagne drink in stemmed glasses or punch cups. For nondrinkers and kids, substitute a 750-milliliter bottle of chilled sparkling apple cider or 3⅓ cups chilled carbonated water for the champagne.

Menu

Holiday Brunch

Often it's hard to find time to entertain during the holidays because your calendar is filled with evening festivities. The solution is simple. Invite family and friends to an elegant brunch. They'll welcome the chance to relax over a luscious meal.

**Ham Soufflé Roll
with Parsley Sauce**
(see recipes, pages 76 and 77)

MENU

Citrus Eye-Opener
(see recipe, page 72)

Ham Soufflé Roll
with Parsley Sauce

Graham Muffins

Festive Fruit

Coffee *or* Tea

Graham Muffins
(see recipe, page 78)

Festive Fruit
(see recipe, page 78)

Holiday Brunch

MENU

Citrus Eye-Opener
  (see recipe, page 72)
Ham Soufflé Roll with
  Parsley Sauce
Graham Muffins
Festive Fruit
Coffee *or* Tea

MENU COUNTDOWN

1 Day Ahead:
Prepare Ham Soufflé and
Parsley Sauce; cover and
chill soufflé and sauce
separately. Prepare batter
for the Graham Muffins;
cover and chill. Prepare
Festive Fruit. Cover. Chill;
stir fruit occasionally.
50 Minutes Ahead:
Preheat the oven.
Combine all ingredients
for the Citrus Eye-
Opener, *except* the
carbonated water; chill till
serving time.

40 Minutes Ahead:
Place soufflé in the oven.
25 Minutes Ahead:
Stir batter and bake the
muffins.
15 Minutes Ahead:
Prepare the coffee or tea.
Transfer fruit to serving bowl;
garnish with kiwi fruit.
10 Minutes Ahead:
Cook sauce for the soufflé.
Just Before Serving:
Add the carbonated water to
the Eye-Opener. Transfer
soufflé to platter and garnish.
Pour sauce into serving bowl.

Parsley Sauce

Pictured on pages 74 and 75.

½ **cup lightly packed parsley**
  sprigs
2 **shallots *or* green onions,**
  cut up (¼ cup)
1 **teaspoon dried basil,**
  crushed
1½ **cups whipping cream**
1 **tablespoon cornstarch**
1 **tablespoon Dijon-style**
  mustard

● In a blender container or food
processor bowl combine parsley, shallots
or onions, and basil. Cover; blend or
process till finely chopped. Add cream,
cornstarch, and mustard. Cover; blend or
process till mixture thickens just slightly
(about 30 seconds). *Be careful not to
overblend.* Transfer mixture to a screw-
top jar. Cover; chill for up to 24 hours.

● When ready to serve, shake sauce in
the jar. Transfer mixture to a medium
saucepan. Cook and stir over medium
heat till thickened and bubbly. Cook and
stir 2 minutes more. Serve over Ham
Soufflé Roll. Makes 1⅔ cups sauce.

Nutrition information per tablespoon: 50 calories,
0 g protein, 1 g carbohydrate, 5 g fat, 19 mg
cholesterol, 23 mg sodium, 22 mg potassium.

**Don't blend the cream
mixture too much—you'll
end up with butter.**

Ham Soufflé Roll

Pictured on pages 74 and 75.

¼ cup margarine *or* butter
½ cup all-purpose flour
⅛ teaspoon pepper
2 cups milk
6 beaten egg yolks
	● Line a 15x10x1-inch baking pan with foil, extending foil 1 inch beyond edges of pan. Grease and lightly flour the foil.
	  In a medium saucepan melt margarine or butter. Stir in flour and pepper. Add milk all at once. Cook and stir till mixture is thickened and bubbly. Remove from heat. Cool slightly.
	  In a medium bowl *slowly* stir thickened mixture into egg yolks.

6 egg whites ¼ teaspoon cream of tartar	● In a large bowl beat egg whites and cream of tartar till stiff peaks form (tips stand straight). Fold a little of the beaten whites into the yolk mixture. Fold the yolk mixture into the remaining beaten egg whites. Spread in the prepared pan. Bake in a 375° oven about 20 minutes or till the soufflé is puffed and slightly set and a knife comes out clean.
6 ounces thinly sliced ham 6 ounces thinly sliced provolone *or* Swiss cheese	● Meanwhile, place a long piece of heavy foil (about 22x18 inches) on a large baking sheet. Generously grease the foil. Immediately loosen the baked soufflé from the pan. Place the foil-lined baking sheet over the soufflé. Invert soufflé onto the foil-lined baking sheet. Carefully peel off foil on top of soufflé. Place ham and cheese in a thin layer on top of soufflé. Use foil on the baking sheet to lift and help roll up soufflé from one of the short sides (see photo, above). Lift soufflé roll with the foil into a 13x9x2-inch baking pan. Cover roll with the foil. Chill for up to 24 hours.
Parsley Sauce (see recipe, opposite) (optional)	● Before serving, heat soufflé roll, covered with the foil, in a 375° oven about 40 minutes or till heated through. Meanwhile, if desired, cook Parsley Sauce. Unwrap the foil and loosen the ends of the roll where the cheese melted onto the foil. Using the foil, lift soufflé from pan. Use large spatulas to transfer the roll to a warm platter, or lift foil and roll soufflé out onto the serving platter. If desired, drizzle with a little sauce. Garnish with whole cranberries and green onion tops, if desired. To serve, slice with a serrated knife. Serve sauce over slices. Makes 8 servings.

To roll this delicate puff into a pinwheel, turn it out onto greased foil. Add ham and cheese. Then, starting at one of the short sides, lift the foil and allow the soufflé to roll up as shown. (Don't roll the foil inside.)

Nutrition information per serving: 281 calories, 17 g protein, 10 g carbohydrate, 19 g fat, 235 mg cholesterol, 583 mg sodium, 241 mg potassium.

Total Time: 30 minutes

Graham Muffins

Pictured on pages 74 and 75.

1⅓	cups finely crushed graham crackers
1¼	cups all-purpose flour
½	cup sugar
1	teaspoon baking powder
¾	teaspoon baking soda

● Grease 16 muffin cups or line with paper bake cups; set aside.

In a medium mixing bowl combine graham crackers, flour, sugar, baking powder, and baking soda. Make a well in the center of the dry ingredients.

Instead of preparing the muffin batter ahead as suggested in this menu, you also can bake the muffins immediately. Just reduce the baking time to 15 to 18 minutes.

1	beaten egg*
1	cup milk*
⅓	cup cooking oil*
½	cup chopped pecans
	Pecan pieces

● In a bowl combine egg, milk, and oil. Add all at once to dry ingredients. Stir just till moistened. Stir in chopped nuts. Store tightly covered in the refrigerator for up to 24 hours.

To bake, stir batter. Fill muffin cups ⅔ full. Place a pecan piece atop each. Bake in a 375° oven about 20 minutes or till golden. Remove from cups. Makes 16.

Nutrition information per muffin: 171 calories, 3 g protein, 20 g carbohydrate, 9 g fat, 18 mg cholesterol, 130 mg sodium, 83 mg potassium.

Note: To reduce calories, fat, and cholesterol, substitute 2 slightly beaten *egg whites* for the whole egg, use *skim milk,* and reduce cooking oil to ¼ cup. (156 calories, 7 g fat, 0 mg cholesterol per muffin)

Festive Fruit

Pictured on pages 74 and 75.

1	cup cranberries (4 ounces)
1	cup water
½	cup sugar
¼	cup currants
1	tablespoon grenadine syrup
2	teaspoons lemon juice
3	medium red apples, cored and cut into thin wedges (3 cups)

● In a large saucepan stir together the cranberries, water, sugar, currants, grenadine syrup, and lemon juice. Bring to boiling, then reduce heat. Cook and stir over medium heat about 5 minutes or till the mixture reaches the consistency of a thin syrup. Add apples; cook 2 minutes more.

Serve the colorful fruit mixture in small sauce dishes or spoon it into Bibb lettuce cups.

2	pears, cored and cut into bite-size pieces
1	kiwi fruit, peeled and sliced

● Remove cranberry mixture from heat. Gently stir in pears. Cool mixture, then transfer to a bowl. Cover; chill in the refrigerator for up to 24 hours. Stir occasionally. To serve, halve kiwi fruit slices; garnish chilled mixture. Serves 8.

Nutrition information per serving: 119 calories, 0 g protein, 31 g carbohydrate, 0 g fat, 0 mg cholesterol, 2 mg sodium, 159 mg potassium.